FITTER FIRST YEAR MCQ

OBJECTIVE QUESTION ANSWERS

MANOJ DOLE

Digitization is the need of the time. In the future, training in industrial training institutes will need to be conducted using online internet to make training more convenient and easy. E-books containing a set of MCQ questions will be made available to the trainees as they need to be more accustomed to the multiple choice questions MCQ to prepare for the online exams taking place in their industrial training institutes.

With all these factors in mind, Mr. Manoj Madhukar Dole Instructor, Industrial Training Institute, Satara, has written books according to the new annual system and NSQF-5 syllabus. And they've created theoretical mobile apps and blogs to make training easier, and made all these educational materials available for download on the world famous websites Google Play Store, Amazon and Apple Book Store.

The books were published by Hon'ble Joint Director Shri Rajendra Ghume Saheb Regional Office of Vocational Education and Training, Pune on 9/1/2019, at this time Shri Prakash Saigavkar Saheb Principal Government Industrial Training Institute Aundh Pune, Shri Tukaram Misal Saheb Principal Govt. Q. Sanstha Satara, Shri Sachin Dhumal Saheb District Vocational Education and Training Officer Satara, Shri Yatin Pargaonkar Saheb Principal Govt. Q. Sanstha Kolhapur, Shri Vikas Teke Saheb Inspector Vocational Education and Training Regional Office Pune, Palekar Foods Products Pvt. Ltd. Entrepreneurial Chairman of Satara Mr. Nilkanthrao Palekar Saheb, Chairman of Hira Foods Mr. Ibrahim Baba Tamboli Saheb, Mrs. Shalmali Pawar Headmaster Government Technical School Center Satara and other dignitaries were present on the occasion

Contents

Prologue

Fitter First Year MCQ is a simple Book for ITI & Engineering Course Fitter, First Year, Sem- 1 & 2, Revised NSQ F-5 Syllabus in 2022, It contains objective questions with underlined & bold correct answers MCQ covering all topics including all about the latest & Important about sawing, filing, marking, chipping, measurement, riveting, soldering, brazing, drilling, OSH&E, PPE, Fire extinguisher, First Aid and in addition 5S, Sheet Metal, Welding (Gas & Arc) which leads to multi-skilling, Different drilling operations (through, blind, angular), reaming, offhand grinding, tapping, dieing, different fits viz., sliding fit, etc., scraping, fastening (nuts & bolts, riveting, studs, screws, etc.,)., Different turning operations on lathe (step, grooving, chamfering, drilling, boring, knurling & threading), simple repair, overhauling and lubrication work on machine and lots more.

We add new question answers with each new version. Please email us in case of any errors/omissions. This is arguably the largest and best Book for All engineering multiple choice questions and answers.

As a student you can use it for your exam prep. This Book is also useful for professors to refresh material.

Foreword

Vocational education and training is imparted through the Department of Vocational Education and Training through the Department of Business Education and Business Practical to supply multi-skilled artisans in line with the rapidly growing demand in the industrial sector in the 21st century. All the occupations within the institutions are important, as the trainees from these occupations develop multi-skills as per the demands of the industry.

with the noble intention of making available MCQ e-books suitable for all businesses, considering that all the examinations in all the industries in the industrial sector are conducted online and include MCQ method questions. Mr. Manoj Madhukar Dole has written a very good e-book on MCQ method as per the new annual syllabus. This e-book will definitely be a guide for all the trainees, trainee candidates, training instructors and others concerned.

The author of the book is Mr. Manoj Madhukar Dole, Instructor Gov. ITI Satara has 17 years of training experience. Written as a new annual pattern, this e-book incorporates modern digital QR Code technology to understand the layout, simple language, and simple syntax, diagrams and videos for each subject. So I am sure that this e-book will definitely be useful for in-depth study and exam practice. The work they have done is certainly commendable.

Mr. Tukaram Misal
Principal Government Industrial Training Institute Satara.

Preface

DGET New Delhi and CSTARI Kolkata have been implementing an annual pattern for all businesses in ITI since the August 2018 session. The examination system will also be changed and it will be online from this year and since all the questions are of Objective Type (MCQ), the trainees are in dire need of in-depth study. It is with this in mind that we are delighted to present the books based on the old NIMI pattern and a complete overview of the new annual pattern, and we hope that these books will be a guide for all business directors and trainees. Is.

For writing these books, Johar Awate Saheb, Principal of ITI Akluj. Former Principal of ITI Satara Saigavkar Saheb, Assistant Director Shri Chandrakant Dhekne Saheb Regional Office of Vocational Education and Training, Pune, District Vocational Education and Training Officer Sachin Dhumal Saheb and Headmaster Government Technical School Kendra Shalmali Pawar Madam and son Adhiraj Dole, mother Kusum Dole, I am very grateful to my father Madhukar Dole and wife Ashwini Dole for their special guidance and cooperation from time to time.

Also, in a very short period of time, the book was reviewed by Shri Rajendra Ghume Saheb, Joint Director, Vocational Education and Training Regional Office, Pune, for his invaluable time in publishing the book. I am sincerely grateful for their feedback.

I am grateful to the Instructor of ITI Satara for there continuous support from the very beginning of writing the book.

From this book, I consider myself blessed to have shared my thoughts on e-learning with you. I will not claim that this book is perfect, because considering the perfection, this book is an attempt and is in its infancy. They will be valuable for improvement if they are tested and suggested.

Manoj Dole
Dated 9/1/2019

Acknowledgements

The industrial training and theoretical examination system of our industrial training institutes and these changes have been accepted by the craft instructors and the trainees. Theoretical examinations conducted in your industrial training institutes are also conducted online. Since these examinations are of multiple choice MCQ method, the trainees will need to get more practice of such questions.

With all these considerations in mind, Mr. Manoj Madhukar, Director, Dole Crafts, Katari Industrial Training Institute, Satara, has done a thorough study and with his diligent work and added his keen intellect, according to the new annual system and NSQF-5 syllabus, e-book of Katari and other machine trades. -Book) and they have created mobile apps and blogs on theoretical topics to make training easier and have made all these educational materials available for download on the world famous websites Google Play Store, Amazon and Apple Book Store. Training has been made easier by creating a print version and using advanced techniques like QR Code.

All these educational materials will definitely be a guide for all the trainees for in-depth study and for the craft instructors and other concerned who are imparting vocational training.

CHAPTER ONE

Fitter First Year MCQ Drawings

www.itibook.com

www.itigov.blogspot.com   www.jobapprentices.blogspot.com   www.ititests.blogspot.com

www.itibook.com

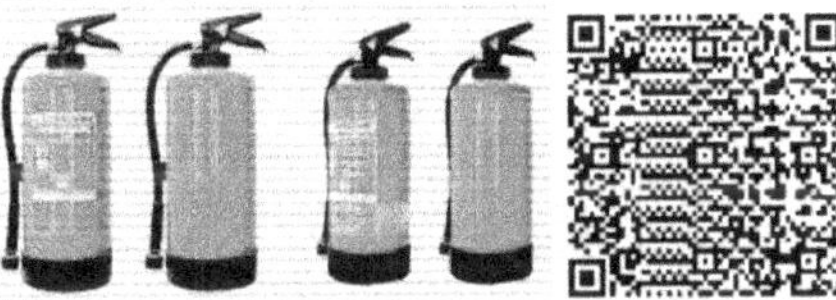
Fire extinguisher

Calliper

www.itibook.com

Hacksaw frame

Universal surface guage

Hammer

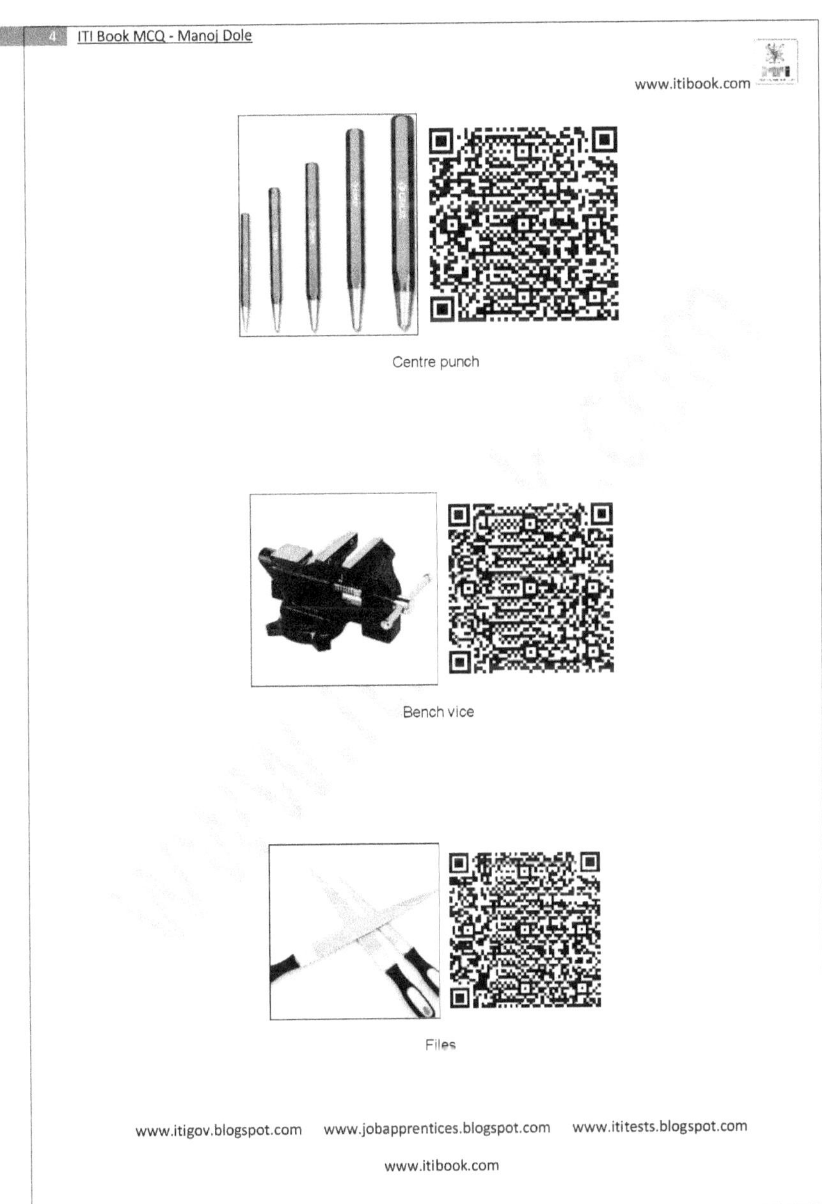

Centre punch

Bench vice

Files

Scraper

Surface Plate

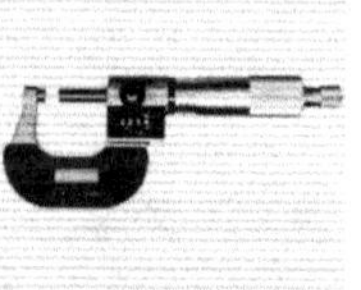

Outside Micrometer

www.itigov.blogspot.com   www.jobapprentices.blogspot.com   www.ititests.blogspot.com

www.itibook.com

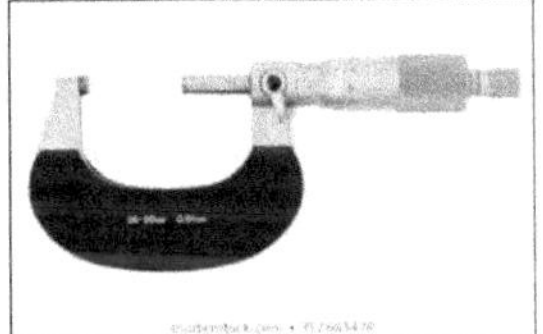

Micrometer

Depth micrometer

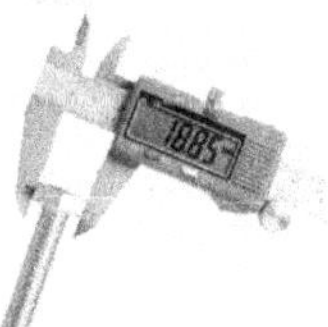

Vernier Calliper

Vernier bevel protractor

www.itibook.com

Drilling

Reamer

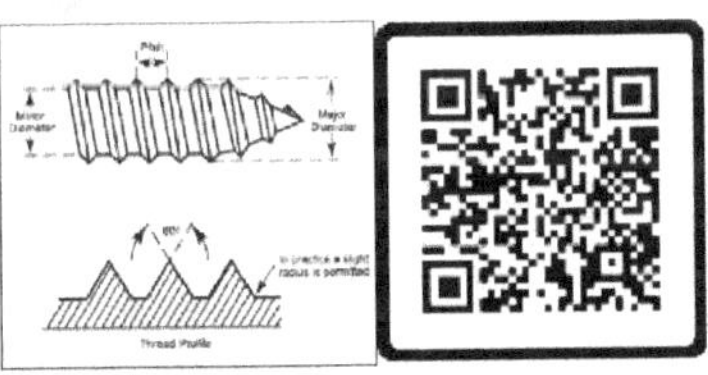

Thread

Tap Die

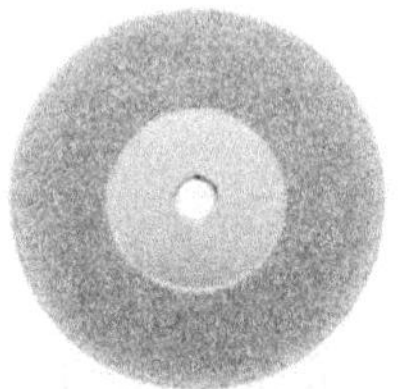

Grinding Wheel

Slip gauge

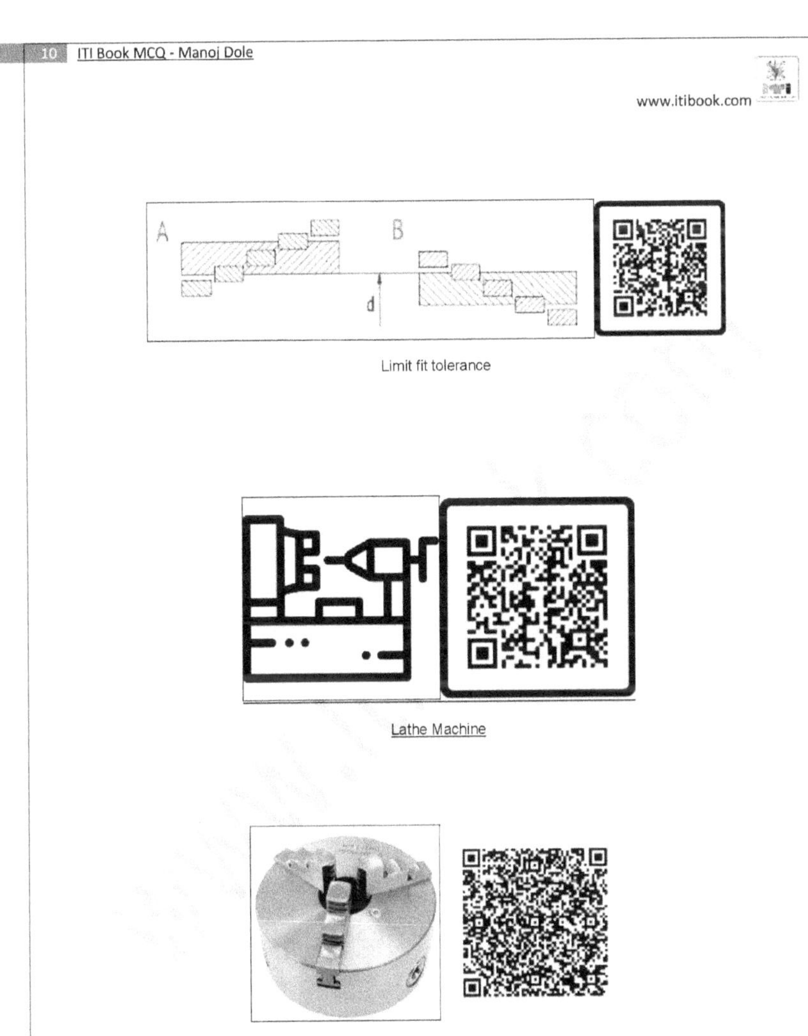

Limit fit tolerance

Lathe Machine

Lathe chuck

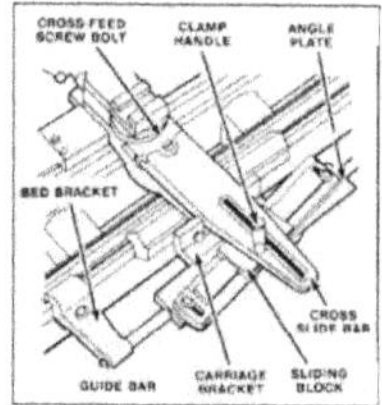

Taper turning attachment

taper ring gauge

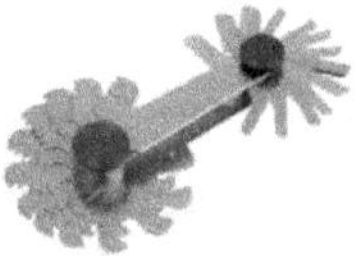

screw pitch gauge

Gear

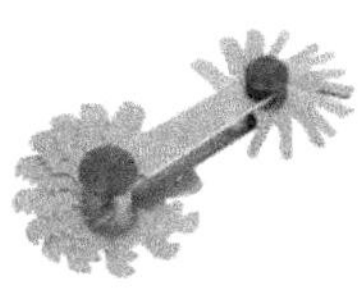

screw pitch gauge

Tap Die

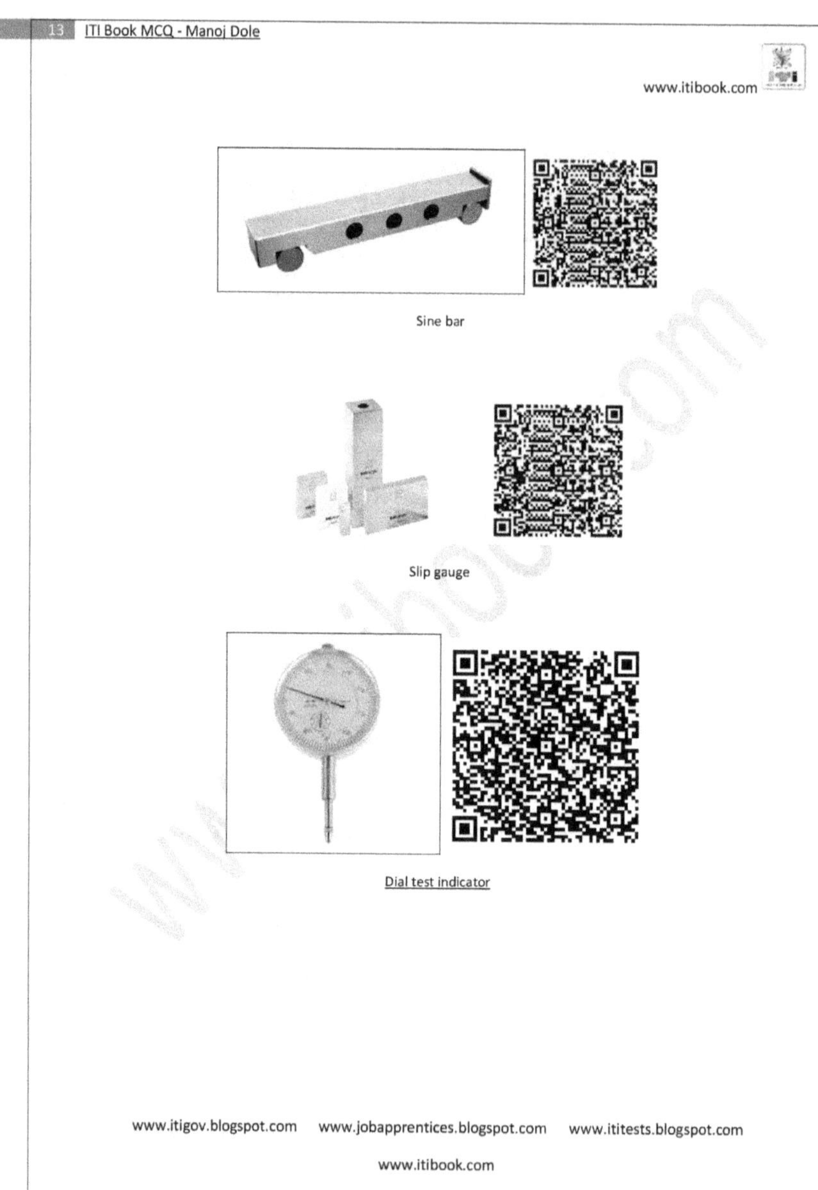

Sine bar

Slip gauge

Dial test indicator

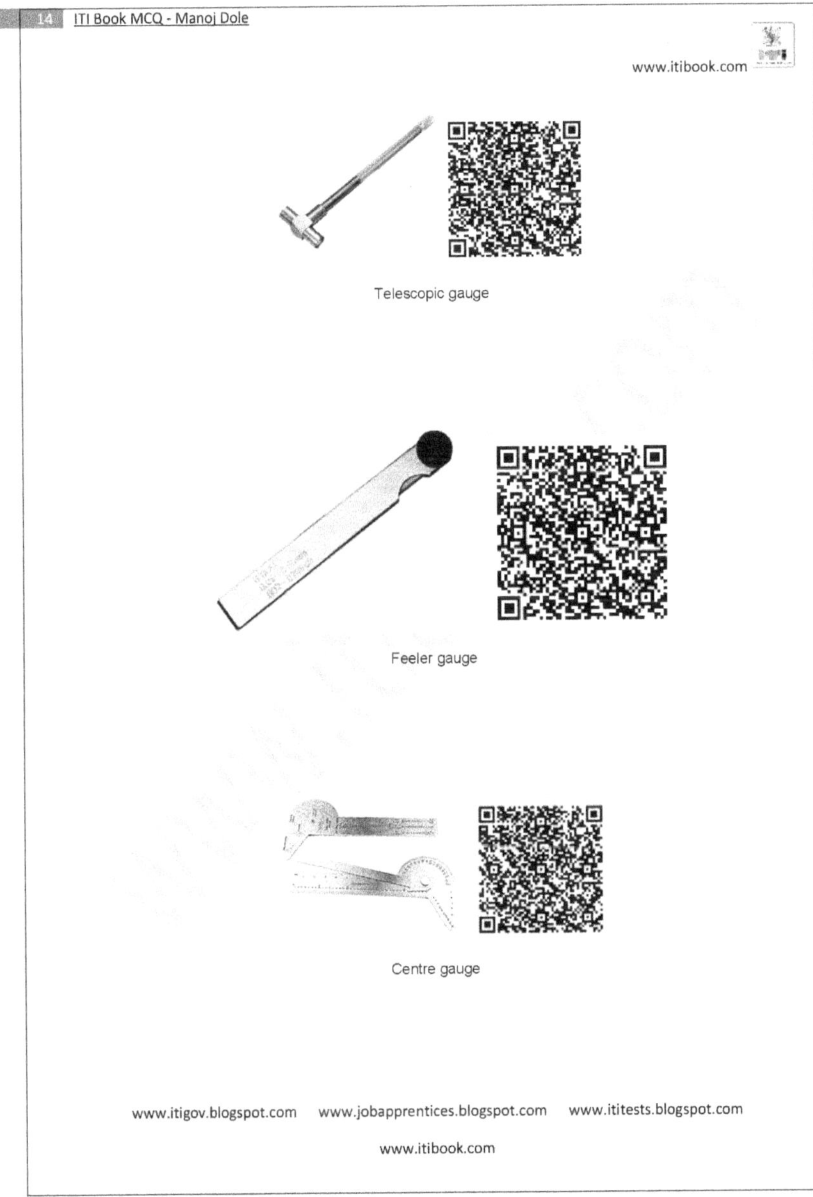

Telescopic gauge

Feeler gauge

Centre gauge

www.itibook.com

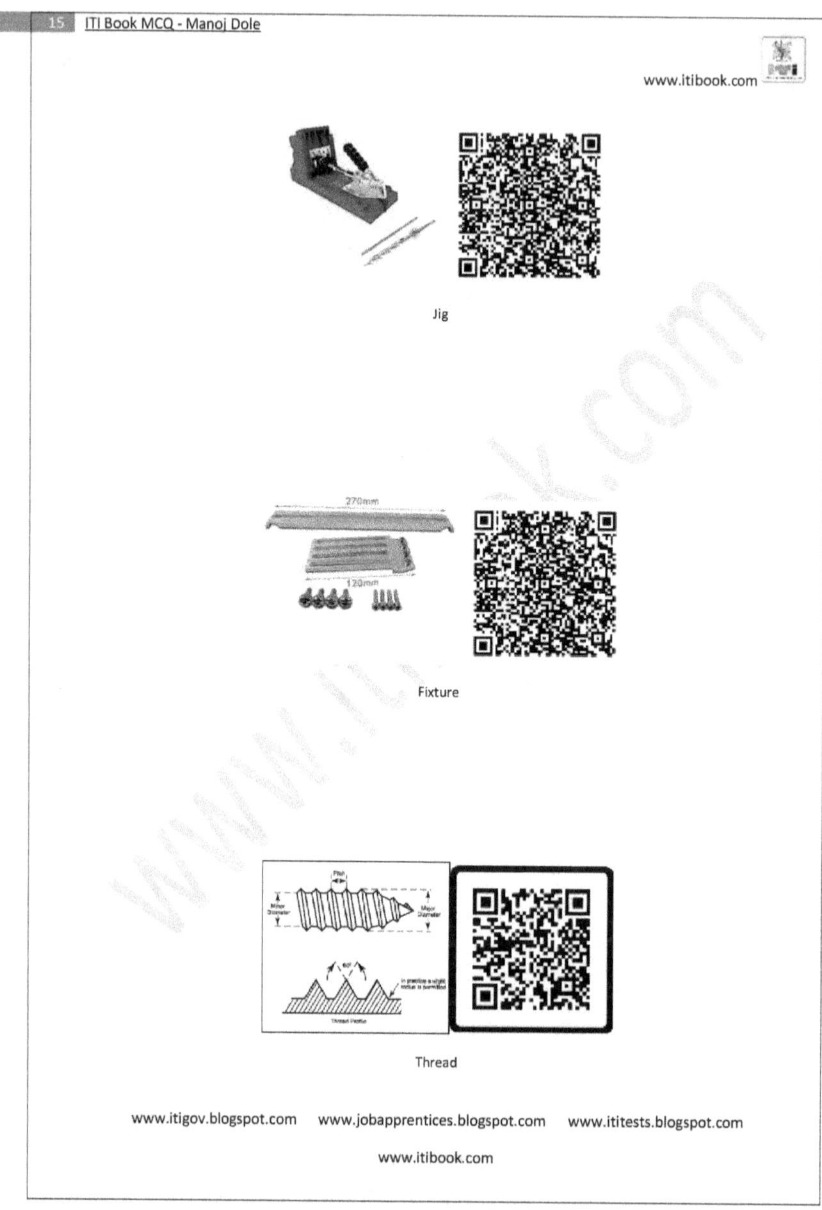

Jig

Fixture

Thread

www.itibook.com

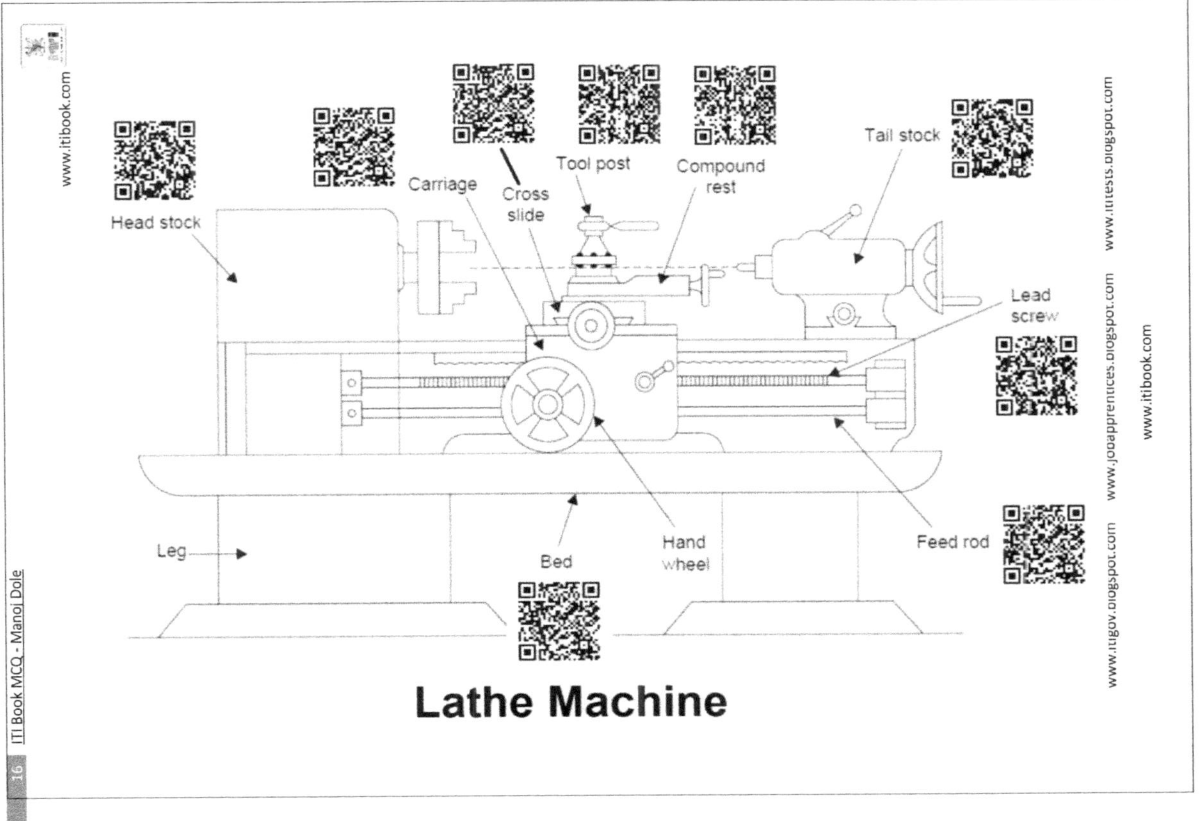

www.itigov.blogspot.com　　www.jobapprentices.blogspot.com　　www.ititests.blogspot.com

www.itibook.com

www.itibook.com

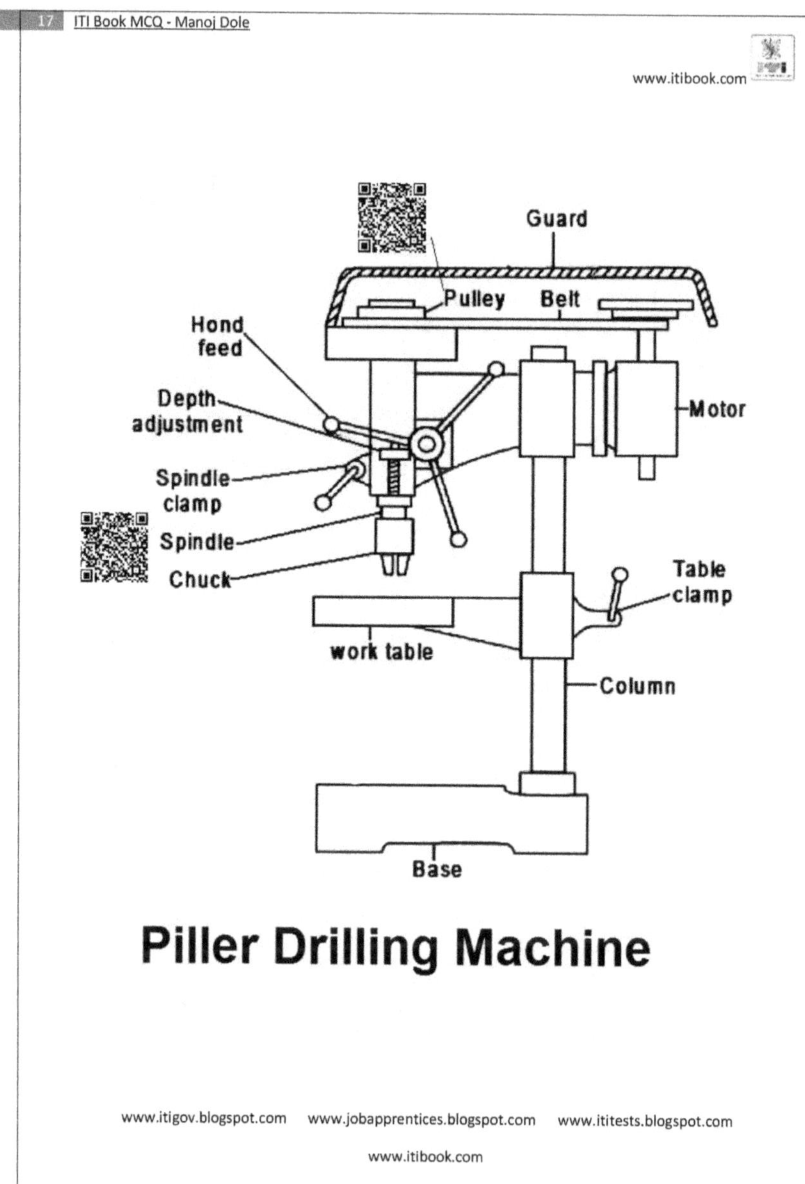

Piller Drilling Machine

www.itibook.com

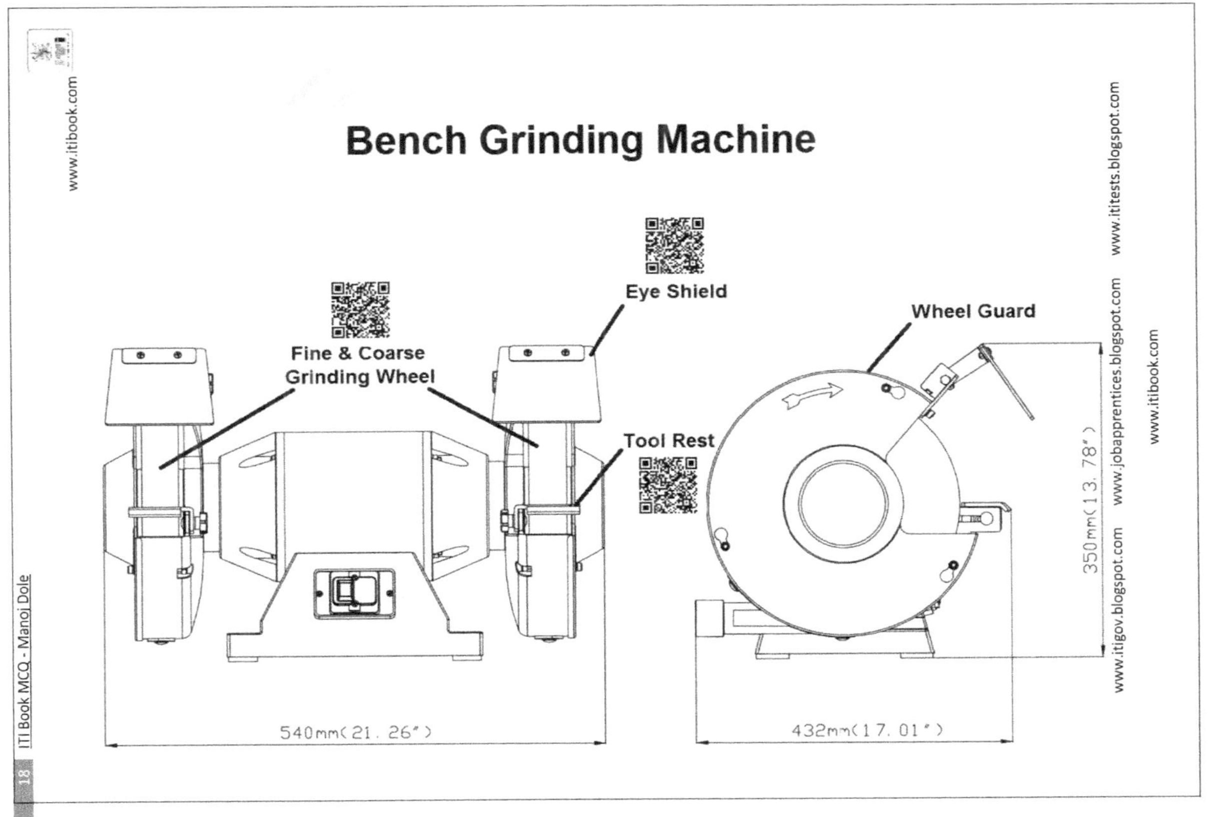

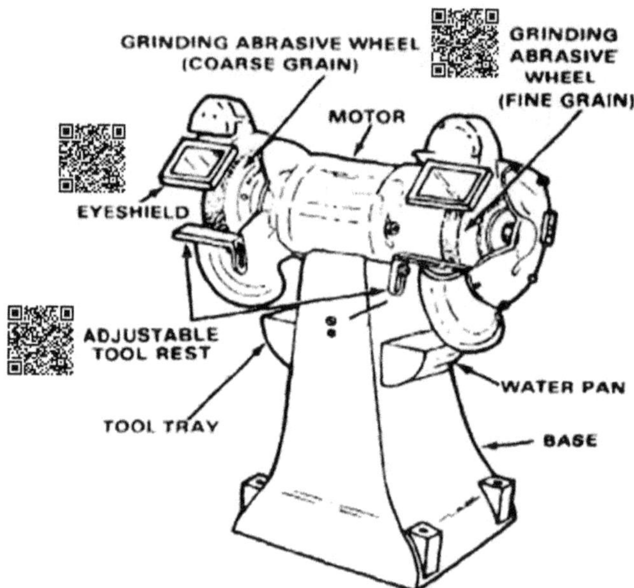

Pedastal Grinding Machine

CHAPTER TWO

Fitter First Year MCQ

1] Which one is a workshop safety?

A] Keep shop floor clean and free from grease, oil or other slippery materials

B] Stop the machine before changing the speed

C] Don't use cracked or chipped tools

D] Don't try to stop a running machine with hand

2] In Personal Protect Equipment (PPE] HELMET is used to

A] protect head

B] Protect eyes

C] Protect hands

D] Protect ears

3] Which of the following belongs to general safety?

A Have a worker in good attitude

B] The work clean and clear

C] Concentrate on your work

D] Keep the floor and gangways clean and clear

4] While grinding, which is used to protect the eyes?

A] Dark green glass

B] Mask

C] Sun glasses

D] Safety goggles

5] Which of the following is done for machine safety?

A] Check the oil level before starting the machine

B] Do things in a methodical way

C] Keep the floor and gangways clean and clear

D] Don't use dies and scarves

6] In Personal Protect Equipment (PPE], 'sleeves' is used to protect

----

A] Face

B] Eyes

C] Ears

D] Hands

7] ABC stands for --------------

A] Automatic Breathing Control

B] Automatic Blood Control

C] Airway Breathing Circulation

D] Automatic Blood Circulation

8] Fire & FIRE EXTINGUISHERS

Fire extinguisher

9] To put off"Class B" fire, the types of fire extinguisher used is ....

A] dry power

B] Carbon dioxide

C] Jet of water

D] Foam type

10] Which type of fire extinguisher is used to put off general fire?

A] Water type Extinguisher

B] Foam type Extinguisher

C] Dry chemical powder Extinguisher

D] Carbon dioxide (C02] Extinguisher

11] In case of bleeding, take treatment Of

D] cold 3" and rest

A] spray cold water

B] Bandage immediately -----.

B] Enquire about the accident thought treatment

12] in case of an accident, the victim should im

A] Asked to take rest

C] Attended immediately

D] leave him

13] First aid is given to an injured or ill person primarily....

A] Save life

B] Prevent further deterioration of the muff's

C] Give best possible comfort

D] All of these

14] Colour code for Bins for waste paper segregation is -----

A] blue Colour

B] Yellow Colour

C] Red Colour

D] Green Colour

15] In Japanese Seiko stands for --------------

A] Shine

B] Sort

C] Standardize

D] Sustain

16] Benefit of SS system is ------

A] Increase in productivity

B] Increase in quality

C] Reduction in wastage of time

D] All of these

17] Safety is -----------

A] nobody's business

B] every bodise business

C] Some bodies business

D] The organization business

18] For basic categories of safety signs are available The meaning of"prohibition" sign ----

A] shows it must not be done
B] Shows what must be done
C] Warns the hazard or danger
D] Gives information of safety provision
18] One micrometer (U] is equal to...
A] 0.1mm
B] 0.01mm
C] 0.001mm
D] 0.0001mm
19] The caliper meant for measuring the width of a slot is...
A] Odd leg caliper
B] Outside caliper
C] Jenny caliper
D] Inside calliper

Calliper

20] The size of the dividers are specified by the -----------
A] Total length of legs
B] Distance between the points when fully opened
C] Length of legs without points
D] distance between the pivot and the point
21] The instrument used to mark parallel lines, parallel to the datum edge is -
A] jenny caliper
B] Divider
C] Outside calliper
D] Inside calliper
22] Which one of the following is an indirect measuring tool?
A] Outside caliper
B] Vernier calliper
C] Steel rule

D] Outside micrometer

23] For cutting thin tubing, the most suitable pitch of the hacksaw blade is...

A] 1.8mm

B] 1.4mm

C] 1mm

D] <u>0.8mm</u>

24] For cutting solid brass, the most suitable pitch of the hacksaw blade is...

A] <u>1.8mm</u>

B] 1.4mm

C] 1mm

D] 0.8mm

Hacksaw frame

25] A new hacksaw blade after a few strokes becomes loose because of the...

A] <u>Stretching of the blade</u>

B] Wing-nut threads being worn out

C] Wrong pitch of the blade

D] Improper selection of the set of saws.

26] While cutting small diameter pipes, it is advisable to watch regularly and ensure that...

A] The cut is along the curved line

B] <u>More saw teeth are in contract</u>

C] The work is not overheated

D] Proper balancing of hacksaw is maintained

27] The vice clamps are used to...

A] Protect hard jaws

B] Clamp the work pieces rigidly

C] <u>Protect the finished surfaces</u>

D] Prevent the movable jaw being filed

28] The reference surface during marking is provided by the...

A] Surface gauge

B] Workpiece

C] Drawing of the work

D] <u>Marking table surface</u>

29] The size of an engineer's vice is specified by the...

A] Length of the movable jaw

B] <u>Width of the jaws</u>

C] Height of the vice

D] Maximum opening of the jaws

30] The part of the universal surface gauge which helps to draw a parallel line along a datum edge is the..

A] Rocker arm

B] Snug

C] Fine adjustment screw

D] <u>Guide pins</u>

Universal surface guage

31] Scribers are made of...

A] Mild steel

B] <u>High carbon steel</u>

C] Brass

D] Cast iron

32] Portion of the hammer used for fixing the handle is...

A] Face

B] Peen
C] Cheek
D] <u>Eye hole</u>
33] Weight of the hammer for the marking purpose is...
A] <u>250g</u>
B] 500g
C] 1 kg
D] 2 kgs

Hammer

34] The size of the dividers are specified by the...
A] Total length of the legs
B] Distance between the points when fully opened
C] Length of legs without the points
D] <u>Distance between the pivot and the point</u>
35] The included angle of the groove of 'V' block is always....
A] 45°
B] 60°
C] 90°
D] <u>120°</u>
36] 'V' blocks are available in grades of...
A] <u>A & B</u>
B] A,B & C
C] 1,2 & 3
D] 1 & 2
37] 'V' blocks of grade 'B' are made of
A] <u>Cast iron</u>
B] Mild steel
C] Steel

D] Cast steel

38] Name the punch used to locate the centre.

A] Prick punch 30°

B] Prick punch 60°

C] Centre punch

D] Dot punch

Centre punch

39] The point angle of centre punch is --------

A] 30°

B] 50°

c] 900

D] 1200

40] Punches are used for forming ---------of any shape

A] Holes

B] Mining

C] Knurling

D] Reaming

41] Generally the length of the handle of the vice is ----------

A] 1.5 times the normal size of the vice

B] 2.5 times the normal size of the vice

C] 3.5 times the normal size of the vice

D] 4.5 times the normal size of the vice

Bench vice

42] Bench vice spindle is made of ....
A] mild steel
B] Cast iron
C] Tool steel
D] Bronze
43] The convexity of files helps...
A] To file concave surfaces
B] To file convex surfaces
C] To prevent rounding of edges of work
D] The file to become straight when pressure is applied

Files

44] Which file used for filling wood, leather and other soft material? .
A] Single cut file
B] Double cut file
c] Rasp cut file
D] Curved cut file
45] File used is used for ------------
A] Cleaning the work piece

C] Renewing the file teeth
B] <u>cleaning the file teeth</u>
D] Cleaning the chips
46] File card is used to --------
A] Clean the work piece
C] Renew the file teeth
B] <u>Clean the file teeth</u>
47] The point angle of scriber is ----------
A] 30°
B] 60°
C] 5° to 10°
D] <u>12° to 15°</u>
48] The cutting angle for chipping cast iron is...
A] 37.5°
B] 55°
C] <u>60°</u>
D] 90°

49] The chisel will dig into the material when...
A] The rake angle is more
B] The clearance angle is too low
C] <u>The angle of inclination is more</u>
D] The angle of inclination is too low
50] A slight convexity is given to the cutting edge to...
A] Cut curved surfaces
B] Cut sharp corners
C] <u>Prevent digging of the ends</u>
D] Allow the lubricant to enter
51] Surface plates are made of...
A] High grade cast steel
B] <u>Fine-grained cast iron</u>
C] Alloy steels

D] Wrought iron

52] Surface plates are specified by their length and breadth & are in

A] decimetre

B] Cubic meter

C] Cylindrical

53] Ribs are given on the unmachined portion of the angle plate for...

A] Easy handling

B] Convenience in manufacturing

C] Clamping while setting on machines

D] Rigidity and to prevent distortion

54] The slots on the angle plate are given for...

A] Reducing weight

B] Aligning the work

C] Lifting using hooks

D] Accommodating bolts.

55] The size of the angle plates is stated by...

A] Weight

B] Length

C] Length x width

D] Size number

56] for high speed parting off work on material like cemented carbide Is'

A] Do all machine

B] Cutting off machine

C] Heavy duty power saw

D] Mining machine sitting saw

57] Gun metal is an alloy of copper, ------------

A] tin and zinc

B] Lead and zinc

C] Zinc and nickel

D] Lead and nickel

58] Cast iron is used for manufacturing machine beds because -------

A] it can resist more compressive stress
B] it is heavy in weight
C] It is cheaper metal
D] It is a brittle metal
59] Accuracy or least count of a metric outside micrometric is ---------
A] 0-1 mm
B] 0.01 mm
C] 0.001 mm
D] 0.02 mm

60] 1000 microns means -----
A] 1 mm
B] 1 m
C] 1000 mm
D] 10 cm
61] in a metric micrometer, a complete revolution of thimble advances
----
A] 0.01 mm
B] 0.25 mm
C] 0.50 mm
D] 1.00mm

Micrometer

62] Ratchet Stop in the micrometer helps to -----------

A] Control the pressure

B] lock the spindle

C] Adjust the zero error

D] Hold the work piece

63] 1000 micron means ------------

A] 1 mm

B] 1 m

C] 1000 mm

D] 10 cm

64] What is the zero reading of a 50-75 mm outside micrometer?

A] 0.000 mm

B] 0.01 mm

C] 25.00 mm

D] 50.00 mm

65] The value of the smallest division on sleeve of a metric outside micrometer is -----

A] 0.50 mm

B] 1.00 mm

C] 1.50 mm

D] 2.00 mm

66] Ratchet stop in the micrometer helps to ---------

A] control the pressure

B] Lock the spindle

C] Adjust the zero error

D] Hold the work piece

67] Least count of depth micrometer is

A] 0.5 mm

B] 0.2 mm

C] 0.001 mm

D] 0.01 mm

Depth micrometer

68] The least count of vernier calliper is (main scale = 49 division, vernier scale = 50 division]

A] 0.1 mm

B] 0.01 mm

C] 0.001 mm

D] 0.02 mm

Vernier Calliper

69] The type of measurement made by using a Vernier Calliper is -------

A] Direct measurement

B] Indirect measurement

C] 90"] (a] 81 (b]

D] None of these

70] The least count of a vernier bevel protractor is...

A] 1"

B] 5'

C] 1∘

D] 5 ∘

71] The part of a vernier bevel protractor which is normally used as a reference base for measuring angles is the...

A] Blade

B] <u>Stock</u>

C] Disc

C] Main scale

Vernier bevel protractor

72] The part of a vernier bevel protector on which main scale divisions are marked is the...

A] Stock

B] Dial

C] <u>Disc</u>

D] Adjustable blade

73] The part of a bevel protractor, which comes in contact with the inclined surface while measuring is the...

A] <u>Blade</u>

B] Stock

C] Disc

D] Dial

74] The value of each division of the main scale of a vernier bevel protractor is...

A] 5'

B] <u>1°</u>

C] 5°

D]10°

75] The value of each division of the vernier scale of a bevel protractor is...

A] 1°

B] 1∘5'

C] <u>1∘55'</u>

D] 5'

76] The taper shank drills are held on the machine by means of...

A] Chucks

B] <u>Sleeves</u>

C] Drift

D] Vice

77] Drill chucks are fitted on the drilling machine spindle by means of a...

A] Knurled ring

B] <u>Arbor</u>

C] Drift

D] Pinion and key

78] The Morse taper provided on drills ranges between...

A] <u>MT 1 to MT 5</u>

B] MT 1 to MT 4

C] MT 0 to MT 5

D] MT 0 to MT 4

79] A drift is used for...

A] Drawing a drill location

B] Fixing chuck on the machine spindle

C] Removing a broken drill from the work

D] <u>Removing the drill from the machine spindle</u>

80] When the taper shank of the drill is larger than the machine spindle, the device to hold the drill is a...

A] Drill sleeve

B] <u>Taper socket</u>

C] Drill drift

D] Chuck and key

81] The suitable cutting fluid for drilling mild steel in a drilling machine is...

A] Synthetic soluble oil

B] Neat oil

C] Distilled water

D] <u>Soluble oil</u>

82] A special feature of the radial drilling machine is...

A] It can be used for drilling with a H.S.S. drill

B] Table can be moved and set at any position

C] A variety of speeds is available

D] <u>The spindle can be brought to any position</u>

83] The point angle of drills depends on...

A] The size of the drill

B] The type of machine

C] <u>The material of the work</u>

D] The RPM of the drill

84] The point angle for a standard drill is...

A] 60°

B] 108°

C] <u>118°</u>

D] 135°

85] The helical angle determines the...

A] Cutting angle

B] Chew angle

C] <u>Rake angle</u>

D] Lip angle

86] The clearance angle of the drill is between...

A] 3° to 5°

B] <u>8° to 12°</u>

C] 12° to 20°

D] 15° to 20°

87] In a remote place (no electricity available] a rail track is to be drilled. Choose the right drilling machine

A] Radial drilling machine

B] Pillar drilling machine

C] <u>Ratchet drilling machine</u>

D] Sensitive drilling Machine

Drilling

88] A drilling machine used by a carpenter for cabinet making is a...

A] Ratchet drilling machine

B] Radial drilling machine

C] <u>Breast drilling machine</u>

D] Sensitive drilling machine

89] Which one of the following drilling machines is used for drilling holes where electricity is not available?

A] Bench drilling machine

B] Pillar drilling machine

C] Redial drilling machine

D] <u>Ratchet drilling machine</u>

90] Which one of the following drilling machine is used for heavy duty work?

A] Bench drilling machine

B] Pillar drilling machine

C] <u>Radial drilling machine</u>

D] Electric hand drilling machine

91] Drill chuck are held on the machine spindle by means of ------

A] <u>arbor</u>

B] Drift

C] draw-in bar

D] Chuck nut

92] Different speeds are obtained in a sensitive bench drilling machine by ----

A] Belt pulley mechanism

B] Hydraulic mechanism

C] Rack and Pinion mechanism

D] Cam and follower mechanism

93] The process of heating and cooling to change the structure of steel for obtaining the required properties is called

A] Hardening

B] Normalizing

C] Heat treatment

D] Tempering

94] The main purpose of annealing is to

A] Increase the hardness

B] Increase the toughness

C] Improve machinability

D] Improve distortion

95] The purpose of normalizing steel is to -----------

A] Remove the induced Stress

B] Improve genes and reduce brittleness

C] Soften the metal

D] Increase the surface?

96] Which one of the following process is used for hardenmg the outer 5" Annealing

A] Hardening

B] Tempering

C] Case Hardening

D] Tear surface

97] The purpose of producmg a component with tough and ductIIe core and hard ou is known as......

A] Hardening

B] Case hardening

C] Tempering

D] annealing

98] Lower critical temperature of high carbon steel while hardening is ----------

A] 9600C

B] 900°C

c] 7230 c

D] 56O C

99] The process of Changing the structure and thus changing the properties by heating and 'cooling is known as

A] Heat treatment

B] Alloying

C] Tempering

D] None of these

100] For refining the grain structure which one of the following heat treatment processes 'Is adopted.

A] Annealing

B] Hardening

C] Tempering

D] Normalising

101] Annealing is performed on iron and steel ---------

A] To remove internal stresses

B] To reduce hardness

C] To improve machinability

D] All of these

102] Which one of the following does not fall under the stages of heat treatment?

A] Heating

B] Cleaning

C] Quenching

D] Soaking

20] METAL 02

103] Gun metal is an alloy of copper, ------------

A] tin and zinc

B] Lead and zinc

C] Zinc and nickel

D] Lead and nickel

104] for making gutters, roof flashing, hoods etc.

A] Galvanised iron

B] Stainless steel

C] Copper sheet

D] Metal sheets

105] in dairies. food processing, kitchen ware etc.

A] Galvanised iron

B] Stainless steel

C] Copper sheet

D] Metal sheets

106] for making buckets, heating ducts, cabinets etc.

A] Galvanised iron

B] Stainless steel

C] Copper sheet

D] Metal sheets

107] Punching a number of holes in a sheet is known as?

a) Perforating

b) Parting

c) Notching

d) Lancing

108] Shearing the sheet into two or more pieces is known as?

a) Perforating

b) Parting

c) Notching

d) Lancing

109] Removing the pieces from the edge in shearing operation is known as?

a) Perforating

b) Parting

c) Notching

d) Lancing

110] Leaving a tab without removing any material is known as?

a) Perforating

b) Parting

c) Notching

d) Lancing

111] Moving a small straight punch up and down rapidly into a die is done by a process known as?

a) Perforating

b) Parting

c) Nibbling

d) Lancing

112] As the thickness of sheet is increased the clearance needed will also?

a) <u>Increase</u>

b) Decrease

c) No effect

d) First decrease then increase

113] Bevelling is particularly suitable for shearing of?

a) Thin blanks

b) <u>Thick blanks</u>

c) Very thin blanks

d) None of the Mentioned

114] Which of the following is a type of die?

a) Simple dies

b) Progressive dies

c) Compound die

d) <u>All of the Mentioned</u>

115] Which of the following die can perform multiple operations such as blanking, punching, notching etc.?

a) Simple dies

b) <u>Progressive dies</u>

c) Compound die

d) None of the Mentioned

116] As the clearance increases, the punch force required?

a) <u>Decreases</u>

b) Increases

c) Remains same

d) First increases then decrease

117] Maximum temperature for forging H. S. S. is -------------degree.

A] 1200

B] 100

C] <u>1100</u>

D] 1500

118] Main purpose Of annealing is -----------.

A] <u>to improve machinability</u>

B] to improve magnetism

C] to increase hardness

D] to increase toughness

119] The carbon percentage in H.S.S. tool is -------

A] 0.75 to 1.00 %

B] 1.00 to 2.00 00

C] 0.60 to 0.75 %

D] 0.02 to 0.03 %.

120] Which one of the following is the resistance of a metal to elastic deformation?

A] Ductility.

B] Strength

C] Stiffness

D] Toughness

121] in canneries and chemical plants Metal sheets

A] Galvanised iron

B] Stainless steel

C] Copper sheet

D] Metal sheets

122] Alloy steel, good corrosive resistance and welds easily

A] Black iron

B] Galvanised iron

C] Stainless steel

D] Aluminium

123] Cheapest, can be rolled to any desired thickness

A] Black iron

B] Galvanised iron

C] Stainless steel

D] Aluminium

124] Resists against rust bright silvery appearance

A] Black iron

B] Galvanised iron

C] Stainless steel

D] Aluminium

125] Corrodes rapidly. Bluish black appearance

A] Black iron

B] Galvanised iron

C] Stainless steel

D] Aluminium

126] Drill a blind hole equal to half of the diameter of the stud. Insert this tool into the hole and remove the stud by turning this anticlockwise.

A] Prick Punch Method

B] Filing square very mm

C] <u>Using square taper punch</u>

D] Ezy-out method

127] If the stud is broken near to the surface, employ this method to remove the stud.

A] <u>Prick Punch Method</u>

B] Filing square very mm

C] Using square taper punch

D] Ezy-out method

128] When a stud is broken a little above the surface this method is used to remove the stud.

A] Filing square very mm

B] Using square taper punch

C] Ezy-out method

D] <u>Making drill hole</u>

129] To extract the broken stud a special tool is employed in this method.

A] Prick Punch Method

B] Filing square very mm

C] Using square taper punch

D] <u>Ezy-out method</u>

130] File the protruding stud into square form and remove it.

A] Prick Punch Method

B] <u>Filing square very mm</u>

C] Using square taper punch

D] Ezy-out method

131] Ammonium chloride is used as a flux for soldering...

A] <u>steel</u>

B] aluminium

C] galvanized iron

D] stainless steel

132] Soldering of M.S sheets takes place at a temperature of...

A] 150∘C

B] <u>250∘C</u>

C] 400∘C

D] 850∘C

133.] In soldering operation the base metal is...

A.] <u>not heated</u>

B.] heated to 200∘C
C.] heated to 650∘C
D.] heated to red hot condition
134] Rivets for Joining sheets to thick plates.
A] <u>Countersunk head</u>
B] Flat head
C] Pan head
D] Mushroom
135] Rivets for Joining sheet metal.
A] Countersunk head
B] <u>Flat head</u>
C] Pan head
D] Mushroom
136] Rivets for Heavy fabrication work.
A] Countersunk head
B] Flat head
C] <u>Pan head</u>
D] Mushroom
137] Rivets for Reduces the height of rivet head above the meta\ surface
A] Countersunk head
B] Flat head
C] Pan head
D] <u>Mushroom</u>
138] Rivets for commonly used for structural work.
A] Countersunk head
B] Flat head
C] Pan head
D] <u>Snap head</u>
139] The pressure of acetylene gas for gas cutting a 10mm M.S plate is...
A.] <u>0.15 kgf/cm2</u>
B.] 0.5 kgf/cm2
C.] 1.0 kgf/cm2
D.] 1.5 kgf/cm2
140] What size of the cutting nozzle you will select for cutting 10mm thick mild steel?
A.] 0.8 mm
B.] <u>1.2 mm</u>
C.] 1.6 mm

D.] 2.0 mm

141] The angle of filler rod in case of rightward welding technique is...

A.] 10 to 20°

B.] 20 to 30°

C.] <u>30 to 40°</u>

D.] 40 to 50°

142] One of the advantages of the high pressure system of gas welding is...

A.] it is cheaper

B.] <u>it is portable</u>

C.] it is less dangerous

D.] it does not require a skilled welder

143] The function of a gas regulator is...

A.] get different types of flames

B.] mix the gases in the required proportion

C.] change the volume of gas flowing to the blow pipe

D.] <u>set the working pressure</u>

144] For welding a lap fillet joint in vertical position by gas what should be the angle of below pipe to the line of weld?

A.] 30° to 40°

B.] 45°to 50°

C.] 60° to 70°

D.] <u>75° to 80°</u>

145] Which metal pipe should NOT be used for passing acetylene gas in order to avoid explosions?

A.] galvanized iron

B.] stainless steel

C.] mild steel

D.] <u>cooper</u>

146] he percentage of carbon in acetylene gas is...

A.] 99%

B.] <u>92.3%</u>

C.] 89.1%

D.] 85.3%

147] Acetylene gas contains

A.] calcium, carbon and hydrogen

B.] calcium and hydrogen

C.] calcium, carbon, hydrogen and oxygen

D.] <u>carbon and hydrogen</u>

148] In an acetylene purifier the sulphureted and phosphorated hydrogen are removed by...

A.] pumice

B.] water

C.] filter wool

D.] <u>purifying chemicals</u>

149] One of the functions of flux in gas welding is...

A.] <u>dissolve the metal oxides</u>

B.] reduce the melting point of mental

C.] increase the flame temperature

D.] increase the root penetration

150] On which of the following factors, the choice of flux for gas welding depend?

A.] <u>type of material to be joined</u>

B.] type of edge penetration

C.] type of fuel gas

D.] type of flame used

151] The divergence allowance required for gas welding a 300mm long copper butt joint is...

A.] 1 to 2 mm

B.] 2 to 3 mm

C.] <u>3 to 4 mm</u>

D.] 4 to 5 mm

152] The type of edge preparation done for gas welding a 4mm thick copper butt joint is...

A.] single bevel

B.] <u>single V</u>

C.] double V

D.] square

153] The size of nozzle used to gas weld 3.15 mm thick aluminium butt joint is...

A.] 13

B.] 10

C.] 7

D.] <u>5</u>

154] What is the value of preheating temperature for gas welding of aluminium?

A.] 100 to 120∘C

B.] <u>150 to 180∘C</u>

C.] 180 to 200∘C

D.] 210 to 250∘C

155] Name the tool used to make and finish the leak proof joints of a pipe T joint

A.] <u>groover</u>

B.] setting hammer

C.] creasing hammer

D.] round bottom stake

156] The angle of vee groove of a single vee but joint for cast iron welding is...

A.] 60∘

B.] 70∘

C.] 80∘

D.] <u>90∘</u>

157] Shielded metal arc welding is classified under the process of...

A.] electric resistance welding

B.] special welding

C.] <u>electric arc welding</u>

D.] electro gas welding

158] How to specify the size of an electrode holder?

A.] by its weight

B.] by its shape

C.] <u>by its current carrying capacity</u>

D.] by the metal used for making it

159] The current set for a 3.15mm medium coated mild steel electrode is...

A.] 50 to 80 amp

B.] <u>90 to 120 amp</u>

C.] 120 to 150 amp

D.] 150 to 170 amp

160] A long arc is used in...

A.] welding with a low hydrogen electrode

B.] horizontal position

C.] plug or slot welding

D.] cast iron welding

161] If the travel speed of electrode is high, which type of weld defect you will get on a T fillet joint?

A.] overlap

B.] slag inclusion

C.] excessive reinforcement

D.] lack of root penetration

162] Which weld defect occurs on a lap fillet joint due to improper weaving of the electrode in the covering/final run?

A.] crack

B.] undercut

C.] lack of fusion

D.] edge of plate melted off

163] Which one of the following is used in the oxy-arc cutting process?

A.] flux coated solid electrode

B.] bare wire tubular electrode

C.] flux coated tubular electrode

D.] bare tungsten arc cutting electrode

164] The electrode holder in a carbon arc cutting equipment is made up of...

A.] plain carbon steel

B.] galvanized iron

C.] aluminium

D.] copper

165] The taper shank drills are held on the machine by means of...

A. Chucks

B. Sleeves

C. Drift

D. Vice

166] Drill chucks are fitted on the drilling machine spindle by means of a...

A.] Knurled ring

B.] Arbor

C.] Drift

D.] Pinion and key

167] The Morse taper provided on drills ranges between...

A.] <u>MT 1 to MT 5</u>

B.] MT 1 to MT 4

C.] MT 0 to MT 5

D.] MT 0 to MT 4

168] A drift is used for...

A.] Drawing a drill location

B.] Fixing chuck on the machine spindle

C.] Removing a broken drill from the work

D.] <u>Removing the drill from the machine spindle</u>

169] When the taper shank of the drill is larger than the machine spindle, the device to hold the drill is a...

A.] Drill sleeve

B.] <u>Taper socket</u>

C.] Drill drift

D.] Chuck and key

170] The process of enlarging the end of a hole for accommodating the socket screw head is...

A.] Reaming

B.] Spot facing

C.] <u>Counter boring</u>

D.] Counter sinking

171] Appropriate tool used for spot facing operation is...

A.] Reamer

B.] Counter sinks

C.] <u>Fly cutters</u>

D.] Lathe tool

172] Centre drilling is an operation of...

A.] <u>Drilling and countersinking</u>

B.] Drilling and counter boring

C.] Marking the centre location before drilling

D.] Enlarging the diameter of a hole

173] A short reamer with an axial hole used with an arbor or mandrel is called -------

A] Parallel reamer

B] Adjustable reamer

C] Expansion reamer

D] Chucking reamer

Reamer

174] Which one of the following machine reamers is used to correct the misalignment between the reamer axis and the work axis?

A] Floating blade reamer

B] Machine jig reamer.

C] Shell reamer

D] Chucking reamer

175] Tap are re sharpened by grinding -----

A] Hutes

B] Threads

C] Diameter

D] Relief

176] 50 metric coarse thread is designated as M12 x 125 What does '12' indicate?

A] Major diameter

B] Root diameter

C] Pitch diameter

D] Blank diameter

177] find the change gears required to cut a 3 mm pitch on 3 lat ' mm pitch 120

A] Driver / Driven =.455/120

B] Driver/ Driven = 60/120

C] Driver / Driven = 80/120

D] Driver/ Driven 2 40/80 of 5 mm

178] calculate the gears required to cut a 1 5 mm pitch on a lathe havmg lead screw Pitch

A] Driver / Driven -_20/100

B] Driver/ Driven = 30/100

C] Driver / Driven = 40/120

D] Driver/ Driven = 60/120

179] the top surface joining the two sides of adjacent thread is called

A] Crest

B] Root

C] Flank

D] Thread is angle

Thread

180] The included angle of the ISO metric thread is --------

A] 27 1 /2°

B] 30°

C] 55°

D] 60°

181] Which one of the following screw thread forms has an included angle of 55° between the flanks of threads?

A] B. A. Thread

B] Acme thread

C] Buttress threads

D] Knuckle thread

182] Which one of the following is used only for finishing and maintaining correct form of thread?

A] Tap

B] Threading tool

C] Threading chaser

D] Tipped tool

183] The angle 0f lS thread (V shaped] is ----------

A] 29°

B] 47 1/4°

C] 50°

<u>D] 60</u>

184] ln which of the following methods, only external threads are made --------

A] Form tool mEthOd

B] Compound rest method

<u>C] Tailstock offset method</u>

D] Taper turning attachment method.

185] The surface joining the crest and the root of a thread is known as ----

<u>A] Flank</u>

B] Shank

C] Pitch surface

D] All Of these

186] Pitch of a two start thread is 4 mm. Then the lead of the thread is given by -----

A] 4mm

B] 2mm

<u>C] 8mm</u>

D] 6mm

187] The Gear ratio required for cutting a screw thread of 2.5 mm on a lathe having a lead screw pitch using single point cutting tool is ----

<u>A] 1:2</u>

B] 2:1

C] 1:1 mm

188] A die in which more than one cutting operation is per formed in one stroke

A] Piercing die

B] Progressive die

C] Combination die

<u>D] Compound die</u>

189] A die in which cutting and non cutting operations are carried out per stroke.

A] Piercing die

B] Progressive die

<u>C] Combination die</u>

D] Compound die

Tap Die

190] A die in which two or more sequential operations are performed at two or more stations upon the work.

A] Piercing die

B] <u>Progressive die</u>

C] Combination die

D] Compound die

191] A die in which the shape of the punch and die are directly reproduced in the metal with little or no metal flow.

A] Progressive die

B] Combination die

C] Compound die

D] <u>Forming die</u>

192] The die used for producing any shape of holes.

A] <u>Piercing die</u>

B] Progressive die

C] Combination die

D] Compound die

193] Abrasives are classifications into.............

A] <u>Two types</u>

B] Three types

c] One types

D] Four types

194] Grinding wheels made out of---------------- abrasive are most common because of its free and cool cutting action.

A] <u>Aluminium oxide</u>

B] Silicon oxide

C] Ammonium oxide

D] Carbide.

195] Which among the following abrasive is mostly used for cutting off wheels for cutting non metallic materials?

A] Aluminium oxide

B] Silicon carbide

C] Diamond

D] None of above

196] Which abrasive particle is used for grinding tungsten carbide tool insert?

A] Silicon carbide

B] A|203

C] Diamond

D] Corundum

197] Which of the following is the natural abrasive?

A] Aluminium oxide

B] Silicon

C] Boron carbide

D] Corundum

198] Which of the following is the manufactured abrasive?

A] Corundum.

B] Quartz

C] Silicon

D] Emery

199] Which abrasive particle is used for grinding steel fittings?

A] Silicon carbide

B] Aluminium oxide

C] Diamond.

D] boron oxide

200] What kind of abrasive cut of wheel should be used to cut concrete stone and masonry?

A] Silicon

B] Al203

C] Diamond grit

D] Glass

201] Aluminium oxide wheel is used for grinding ------------

A] cast iron

B] Cemented carbide.

C] HSS '

D] ceramic

202] The bond of diamond wheel suitable for offhand grinding of the tipped tool is ....

A] Resinoid

B] Vitrified

C] Shellac

D] Metal

Grinding Wheel

203] Which among the following bonds, is used commonly?

A] Vitrified bond '

B] Rubber bond

C] Shellac bond

D] Silicate bond

204] The symbol conventionally used for resinoid .bond is ~~~~~~~~

A] v

B] R f

C] B

D] E

205] In grinding practice the term "grade of wheel" refers to ---------'

A] Hardness of the abrasive used

B] Strength of the bond of the wheel

C] Finish 0f the Wheel

D] Hardness of the work pieces

206] Which bond is used in cut of wheels?

A] Rubber

B] Vitrified

C] Resirjoid

D] Shellac

207] Hardness of grinding wheel is determine by ----------
A] the resistance exerted. by the bond against grinding Stress
B] Hardness of abrasive grains
C] Hardness of bond
D] Ability to penetration
208] When it is required to run a Grinding wheel safely at very high speed, which bond should be used? "
A] Vitrified
B] Shellac
C] Silicate
D] resinoid' and rubber
209] in surface grinding what is the suitable range of grain size of the grinding wheel for general purpose surface grinding?
A] 20 to 36
B] 46 to 60
C] 80 to 120
D] 150 to 300
210] AS per Indian Standard, the grain '46'.comes under the group of «w. -----
A] Coarse
B] Medium
C] Fine
D] Very fine
211] The grit size of the abrasives used in the grinding wheel is usually specified by ----------
A] Hardness number
B] A size of wheel
C] Softness or hardness of the abrasive
D] Mesh number
212] Bench grinder are used for ....
A] Heavy duty work
B] Heavy and light duty work
C] Light duty work
D] Lather work
213] Bench Grinders are fitted on a ....
A] Base
B] Table.
C] Wheel guards

D] Conveyor

214] Which of the following statement is correct?'

A] Gauges are used to check the size

B] Template are used to chuck-the size

C] Gauges are used to measure the size

D] Gauges are used to check shape of component

215] At what standard temperature are the gauges kept in the section?

A] 100 C

B] 20° C

C] 100 F

D] 20° F

216] Which grade of slip gauge is generally used in workshop?

A] Grade 0

B] Grade l

C] Grade H

D] Grade 0

Slip gauge

217] As per Indian Standards a special set gauge is used consisting of

A] 81 Pieces

B] 112 Pieces

C] 120 Pieces

D] 130 Pieces

218] The accuracy of reference gauge is

A] 0.05 mm

B] 0.01 mm

C] 0.001 .

D] 0.0001 mm

219] In case of ant burr on slip gauge, it should be removed by

A] Filling

B] Lapping

C] Scraping

D] Grinding

220] Hardness of slip gauge should be?

A] More than 63 HRC

B] 58 HRC

C] 55 HRC

D] 50 HRC

221]------------ Slip gauge is used for Checking component within an accuracy of 0.01 mm.

A] Workshop gauge

B] Inspection gauge

C] Reference gauge

D] Ring gauge

222], -----------is used for checking accuracy of precision instrument.

A] Gauge block

B] Fader gauge

C] Sine bar

D] Plug gauge

223] Slip gauge are Cleaned before using to ensure accuracy. What medium will you use for this purpose.

A] Oil

B] Thinner

C] Carbon tetrachloride/ White petrol

D] Turpentine oil

224]To check the dimensional accuracy of identical components, a dial test indicator is set-for t 6 Size and used as a comparator. What will you use toset to the dial test indicator?

A] Dial test indicator

B] Teeter gauge

C] Slip gauge

D], surface gauge

225] Which one of the following is important factor required to achieve the interchange ability in mass production? .

A] Geometrical accuracy.

B] Standardization

C] Dimensional accuracy

D] Surface finish

226] Interchange ability is normally applied for? _

A] Repairing of parts
B] Mass production
C] Single piece production
D] All of these

227] When tolerance given in one side of the basic dimension, it is called --------

A].Tolerance system
B] Unilateral tolerance
C] Bilateral tolerance
D] Allowance System

228] The measured Size Of the dimensions of a component as called---------

A] Basic size
B] Nominal Size
C] Allowed size
D] Actual size

229] In the drawing the dimensions of a shaft is shown 40i 0068/0042, which is the size of Shaft within the tolerance?

A] 4.0.64 mm
B] 40.042 mm
C] 40.000 mm
D] 39.998 mm

230] In Hole basic system ----------

A] The size of the shaft is made constant
B] The Size of the hole is made constant
C] Only 'allowance is given on the hole
D] The permissible tolerance are given on the hole and the Shaft

231] The Size of a component is given as 24 -0.1. What does -O.1 indicates? _

A] Upper deviation is + 0.1 mm .
B] Lower deviation is 0.0 mm
C] Fundamental deviation is 0.0 mm
D] Lower deviation is _0.1 mm

232] The tolerance of a hole iS the difference between the -------

A] Maximum hole Size and maximum Shaft size
B] Maximum hole size and maximum hole Size
C] Minimum'hole size and maximum Shaft Size
D] Minimum hole Size and minimum shaft Size

233] A hole whose lower deviation is zero is called basic hole. Which one of the following letter indicates basic hole?

A] E

B] F

C] G '

D] H

234] Which one having upper deviation zero?

A] Bassc Shaft

B] Basic hole

C] Tolerance

D] Clearance

235] A ball bearing on a shaft is type of fit? ,

A] Clearance fit

B] Driving fit

C] Shrinkage fit

D] None of the above

236] In the BIS system of limits and fits, the grade of tolerance are represented by number Symbols and there are ---------i

A] 14 grades of tolerance

B] 16 grades of tolerance

C] 18 grades of tolerance '

D] 20 grades of tolerance

237] A Product is said to have the quality when ....

Limit fit tolerance

A] Its shape and dimensions are within the

B] It is fit for use

C] It appears to be very good

D] The choice of material is right

238] The maximum clearance required between hole'30 +0.021, 0.000 and shaft 30 -0.110, 0.143 is.

A] 0.110 mm '

B]0.131 mm

C] 0.164 mm

D] 0.143 mm

239] A dimension is stated as 25 .1002 mm in a drawing. What is the tolerance?

A] +0.02 mm'

B] +0.04 mm

C] -0.02 mm

D] 25.00 mm

240] A pin is fitted in a hole. The tolerance zone of the pin is entirely above that of hole. The fit obtained will be?

A] Clearance fit

B] Transition fit

C] Interference fit

D] Running fit

241] Tolerance is given to the part size to............

A] Production the part within the required permissible size error

B] Increase the production

C] Decrease the Production

D] Finish the components approximately

242] Which one of the following is the clearance fit under the whole basic system?

A] 20 H7/p6'

B] 2067/211

C] ZOG/gll .

D] 20H/g11.

243] The three classes of fits as per BIS system aré ....

A] Clearance fit, interference fit and transition fit

B] Medium fit, push fit and tight fit

C] Flat fit, round fit and square fit

D] 'Sliding fit ', loose fit and shrinkage fit

244] Which one of the following tolerance specifications has a maximum dimensionless than 20 mm?

A] 20 +0.2,-0.3

B] 20 320.2

C] 20 -0.2, 0.3 e

D]m 20 +500, ~03

245] Difference between the maximum and minimum limit is --------------------

A] Single informant

B] Basic shaft

C] Clearance

D] Tolerance

246] A shaft 55 running freely in bush bearing the type of fit is ---------

A] Clearance fit

B] Driving plate

C] shrinkage fit

D] None of the above

247] Steel is an alloy of

A.] copper and tin

B.] iron and carbon

C.] tin and lead

D.] zinc and brass

248] The non-ferrous metal amongst the following, which is magnetic is

A.] copper

B.] aluminium

C.] titanium

D. nickel

249] An alloy of copper and zinc produces

A.] white metal

B.] brass

C.] steel

D.] bronze

250] The cutting speed for aluminium with H.S.S. tools is

A.] 30 m/min

B.] 50 m/min

C.] 70 m/min

D.] 130 m/min

251] The cutting speed for brass with a H.S.S. tool is

A.] 10 m/min

B.] 25 m/min

C.] 70 m/min

D.] 140 m/min

252] Used for scraping large flat surfaces.

A] Bull-nose scraper

B] Three-square

C] Half round scraper

D] None of above.

253] Used for scraping small scraper diameter holes and for deburring of holes.

A] Bull-nose scraper

B] Three-square

C] Half round scraper

D] None of above.

254] Used for scraping bearing surfaces which are neither too big nor too small.

A] Bull-nose scraper

B]Three-square

C] Half round scraper

D] None of above.

255] Used for scraping large diameter holes.

A] Bull-nose scraper

B] Three-square

C] Half round scraper

D] None of above.

256] -------------is the COFFEC'E dimension when the micrometer measures 45.54mm, if it is having a negative error of 0.02mm

A] 45.58 mm

B] 45 54 mm

C] 45.56 mm

D] 45.53 mm.

257] When the faces of the anvil and the spindle touch each other if the Zero of the Sleeve scale coincides with the zero of the thimble scale, then it is said to be -----------

A] Positive error

B] Negative error

C] Zero error

D] No error

258] Depth bar is used for measurement of -------------

A] Height.

B] Length

C] Depth

D] Inches

259] The dial test indicator shows the measurement as...

A.] The actual size of the component

B.] The difference between the two steps of 5 mm

C.] The magnified small variations in sizes through a pointer

D.] The direct reading of the dimension

260] V -block and dial indicator method is used to measure the

A] Length of the work piece ground

B] Circularity of the surface of the work piece

C] Flatness of the surface

D] Pitch of the thread

261] Which one of the following is not correct about dial test indicator?

A] It has 100 divisions on its dial

B] Motion of the stem is transferred to the dial through Gear train.

C] Its accuracy is 0.1 mm

D] Used in conjunction with depth gauge

262] Driving plates are used for

A] mounting fixtures and work pieces

B] driving shafts between Centre's with a lathe dog

C] facing operations only

D] internal operations only

263] Balancing is done in the face plate work

A] to increase the speed

B] to reduce the pressure on the tool

C] for uniform rotation of work

D] to get a good finish

264] A face plate is used to hold

A] a round job

B] a finished job

C] an irregular Job

D] a hollow job

265] Which is correct angle plate used with face plate

(A] Solid Type

(B] Box Type

(C] Adjustable Type

(D] None of them

266] Face plate is made from......

(A] Mild Steel

(B] Cast Iron

(C] Brass

(D] Aluminium

267] Which following accessories is use for odd an uneven job turning?

(A] Three Jaw Chuck

(B] Two Jaw Chuck

(C] Driving Plate

(D] Face Plate

268] An irregular shaped work piece is turned on a Lathe. Which one of the following work holding accessories is used?

A] Two Jaw chuck

B] Three Jaw chuck

C] Driving plate

D] Face plate

269]The pads of a steady rest are made of

A] carbon steel

B] lead

C] mild steel

D] brass

270] A steady rest is used

A] to hold jobs

B] for face plate work

C] to drive the job

D] to support the job

271] A follower steady is held on the

A] lathe bed

B] lathe carriage

C] lathe spindle

D] tailstock

272] When turning long work pieces, the following is used

A] sleeve

B] change gear

C] steady rest

D] bracket.
273] How many types of Lathe as per manufacturing?
A] Two
B] Three
C] Four
D] Five

Lathe Machine

274] How many types of Centre Lathe?
A] Two
B] Three
C] Four
D] Five
275] How many types of production lathe?
A] Two
B] Three
C] Four
D] Five
276] Which type of lathe is Roller Lathe?
A] Bench Lathe
B] Special Lathe
C] Production Lathe
D] Centre Lathe
277] For mass-production which machine is used?
A] Centre Lathe
B] Production Lathe
C] Special Lathe
D] Engine Lathe
278] Which lathe is used for more accurate job?

A] Centre Lathe

B] Special Lathe

C] Production Lathe

D] Tool Room Lathe

279] The accuracy of Tool Room Lathe is.... to Compeer Centre Lathe.]

(A] Less

(B] More

(C] Very Less

(D] Equal

280] In Locomotive Assemble Wheel with Axel is turning on ......Lathe

(A] Centre Lathe

(B] Tool Room Lathe

(C] Wheel Lathe

(D] Gap Bed Lathe

281] Which one of the following is used to hold the regular Workpice

A] Faceplate

B] Mandrel

c] Three-Jaw chuck

D] Four-Jaw chuck.

Lathe chuck

282] The threads on the back side of the four Jaw chuck has type...------of threads.

A] Square

3] Trapezoidal

C] V -shape

D] None of these

283] Scroll & gear mechanism is employed in ------------------

A] Collette Chuck

B] Magnetic chucks

C] Three jaw chucks

D] Four jaw chucks

284] The size of Three jaw chuck is specified by ---------

A] The size of each jaw

B] The diameter of body of the chuck

C] Width of the body chuck

D] Thickness of each chuck

285] The magnetic chuck is aligned -----with the traverse of the work table

A] Perpendicular

B] Angular

C] Parallel

D] Parallel and perpendicular

286]The equipment which removes residual magnetism from the ground work piece. .

A] De-magnetizer

B] Electromagnet

C] Permanent magnet

D] None of the above

287] Details to be given to specify a magnetic chuck ----

A] Types whether electromagnetic

B] Length of the chuck

C] Plain vice

D] All of these

288] The limitation of the magnetic chuck is---------

A] Variable holding pressure

B] Longer setup time

C] Difficulty in centring and working with small work piece

D] None of the above

289] The purpose of the demagnetiser, when using a magnetic chuck is to ----

A] Demagnetise the chuck only

C] Demagnetise both the chuck and workpiece

D] None of these

290] Knurling operation is done at the

A] turning spindle speed

B] high spindle speed

C] 1/3 of the turning spindle speed

D] 1/2 of the turning spindle speed

291] Knurling is the operation of

A] shearing

B] forming

C] turning

D] pressing

292] Mandrels are generally used when machining with

A] heavy cuts

B] short facing cuts

C] light cuts

D] boring tools

293] The taper ratio of the morse taper is

A] 1 in 10

B] 1 in 15

C] 1 in 20

D] 1 in 25

294] The morse standard taper is available in

A] 16 Nos

B] 12 Nos

C] 10 Nos

D] 8 Nos

295] Taper turning by offsetting the tailstock method can produce

A] an internal taper

B] an internal taper thread

C] an external taper

D] both external and internal tapers

296] By using the taper turning attachment, tapers can be turned with a setting angle up to

A] 10°

B] 15°

C] 20°

D] 30°

Taper turning attachment

297] The accuracy of a taper is generally checked by means of......

A] <u>taper gauges</u>

B] gauge blocks

C] indicator and height gauge

298] Turning tapers by the compound rest method involves working solely with

A] Decimal measurements

B] fractional measurements

C] metric measurements

D] <u>angular measurements.</u>

299] Long tapers are produced

A] with the taper turning attachment

B] with the compound slide

C] <u>by setting over the tail stock</u>

D] by adjusting the cross slide.

300] The length of turned tapers are checked with

A] <u>vernier calliper</u>

B] micrometer

C] inside callper

D] dial test indicator.

301] The disadvantages of taper turning using the com. pound slide are

A] only long tapers can be turned

B] only very large tapers can be turned

C] only manual in feed is possible

D] <u>only short tapers can be turned due to the restrictions of the compound slide.</u>

302] External tapers are checked with

A] limit plug gauge

B] taper ring gauge

C]taper plug gauge

D] thread plug gauge.

taper ring gauge

303] The use of a taper turned on lathe is ----

A] Assist to transmit drive in the assembled parts

B] Used for Assembly and disassembly of parts

C] Give self alignment in the assembled parts

304] Which type of method is used in mass production of production of producing small length of taper?

A] Form tool

B] Compound slide

C] Tailstock offset.

D] Taper turning attachment

305] Morse standard taper is one of the internationally accepted standards taper, which is available in numbers from--------

A]1to7

B]1 to 8

C] O to 7

D] 0 to 8

306] Which taper turning method is used for cutting steep taper?

A] Set over method

B] Taper turning attachment

C] Form tool

D] Swivelling the compound rest

307] Morse taper is used in which of the following machine components -...

A] Spindles of lathe

B] Spindles of drill machine

C] Shanks of reamers

D] All of these

308] For mass production of the taper which one of the following method is used........

A] Tailstock offset method

B] Taper turning attachment method

C] Form too method

D] Compound slide method

309] The major diameter of the taper is 40 mm, minor diameter is 30 mm. The total length of the job is 100 mm is tapered then offset is given by -

A] 5 mm

B] 7.5 mm

C] 12 mm

D] 9 mm

310] .... & .... Shape job turning in form turning?

A] Plain & V. Shape

B] Squre & Round

C] Concave & Convex

D] V & Round

311] Which part making by form turning of machine?

A] Base

B] Bed

C] Carrage

D] Handles

312] Form turning done for this purpose....?

A] For attractive job

B] for large material cutting

C] for better finishing

D] for smallest cut on job

313] Which type of metal tool use for mass production of form turning?

A] H.S.S.

B] H.C.S.

C] Carbide

D] Cementite

314] A BSW threading tool is to be ground with an included angle of

A] 55°

B] 60°

C] 47.5°

D] 29°

315] The nose radius of a metric 'V' thread tool is

A] <u>0.144 x P</u>

B] 0.25 x P

C] 0.414 x P

D] 0.0144 x P

316] The depth of B.I.S. metric thread is

A] 0.6403 x P

B] 0.6 x P

C] <u>0.6134 x P</u>

D] 0.5 x P

317] Threading tools are checked for accuracy for the 60° angle by using

a

A] Thread plug gauge

B] <u>centre gauge</u>

C] screw pitch gauge

D] tool angle gauge

318] The number of threads per inch can be checked with a

A] tool gauge

B] metric rule by counting

C] ring gauge

D] <u>screw pitch gauge</u>

<u>screw pitch gauge</u>

319] When threading, the carriage is moved along the ways by

A] a gear train on a track

B] the feed rod spline or key-way

C] <u>the lead screw thred</u>

D] the hand wheel

320] Thread chasers are used for

A] quick production of threads
B] <u>maintaining an exact form of thread</u>
C] cutting threads on hard materials
D] cutting threads on soft materials
321] Thread chasers are made out of
A] carbon steel
B] high speed steel
C] <u>tool used</u>
D] stainless steel
322] Chasers are used to cut
A] <u>'V' form threads only</u>
B] square threads only
C] acme threads only
D] any form of threads
323] To cut M24 x 3 mm pitch internal threads, the core diameter of the job is
A] 27.00 mm
B] 24.50 mm
C] <u>21.00 mm</u>
D] 24.00 mm
324] The depth of cut for M24 x 3 mm internal thread is
A] <u>0.5412 x 3</u>
B] 0.6134 x 3
C] 0.5 x 3
D] 0.7 x 3
325] To cut 24 x 3 mm internal acme threads, the core diameter of the job is
A] 20.00 mm
B] 21.66 mm
C] 21.00 mm
D] <u>20.60 mm</u>
326] The depth of cut for metric square threading is
A] 0.6 x P
B] <u>0.5 x P</u>
C] 0.5412 x P
D] 0.6412 x P
327] To cut buttress thread, the depth of cut is
A] 0.5412 x P

B] <u>0.6 x P</u>
C] 0.7 x P
D] 0.75 x P
328] For cutting acme threads, the tool is ground to an included angle of
A] 60°
B] 29°
C] <u>47.5°</u>
D] 30°
329] The half-nut lever is used for
A] engaging the longitudinal feed on the carriage
B] taking up the slack in the cross-slide nut
C] changing from longitudinal to cross-feed
D] <u>threads cutting</u>
330] The bottom surface joining the two sides of adjacent thread (external thread] is...
A] Flank
B] <u>Root</u>
C] Crest
D] Pitch
331] The form of thread used in carpenters vice is...
A] Square
B] Acme thread
C] <u>Sawtooth Thread</u>
D] Knuckle thread
332] Cast iron is used for manufacturing machine beds because -------
<u>A] it can resist more compressive stress</u>
B] it is heavy in weight
C] It is cheaper metal
D] It is a brittle metal
333] Which one of the following operations can't be performed on a Center Lathe? .
A] Turning
B] Thread cutting
C] <u>Gear cutting</u>
D] Taper turning

<u>Gear</u>

334] For carbide tip tool turning on hard material it has.....ecential?

A] Side Rake angle

B] Zero Rake angle

C] Positive Rake angle

D] <u>Negative Rake angle</u>

335] A slot is to be milled in a steel component using a 9 mm diameter slot mill rotating at 373 rpm. The cutting speed will be

A] <u>10.55 m/min</u>

B] 26.7 m/min

C] 181.9 m/min

D] 11 m/min

336] A 12 mm diameter end mill is to be set for a cutting speed of 14 m/min. the r.p.m. to be set on the machine should be

A] 271.7 rpm

B] 183.17 rpm

C] 76 rpm

D] <u>371.21 rpm</u>

337] A cutter has a diameter of 80 mm. if the cutting speed is to be 20 m/min. the rpm of the spindle should be

A] 90.7 rpm

B] <u>79.55 rpm</u>

C] 25.75 rpm

D] 107.95 rpm

338] Zero Rake angle give for tool?

A] To avoid friction of tool

B] <u>For increase tool life</u>

C] For increase straight of tool

D] For better finishing on job

339] Which type of metal tool use for mass production of form turning?

A] H.S.S.

B] H.C.S.

C] Carbide

D] Cementite

340] When cutting tool start his action & cutting force in increase at this position subsequent effect of tool is..?

A] Clearance angle of tool is high

B] Clearance angle of tool is low

C] Rake angle of tool is low

D] Rake angle of tool is high

341] The purpose of Rake angle for tool is?

A] Right direction for mental chips

B] Good finishing on job

C] For increase life of tool

D] For avoid friction in between job & tool

342] The purpose of provide clearance angle for cutting tool is?

A] For right direction of metal cutting chips

B] reduce friction on hit of job

C] for sage of job friction

D] for better finishing on job

343] If cutting tools setting upper centre height done what happen?

A] Encrease top Rake angle

B] less top Rake angle

C] No effect on Top Rake angle

D] Encrease clearance angle

344] What happen if cutting tool setting done lower of center height?

A] Encrease top Rake angle

B] Decrease top Rake angle

C] No any effect on to Rake

D] Decrease clearance angle

345] If cutting tool is upsetting of centre of job?

A] Encrease front clearance angle

B] Decrease front clearance angle

C] no any effect on front clearance angle

D] none of them

346] If cutting tool is down setting of centre of job?

A] Front clearance angle is increase

B] Front clearance angle is decrease

C] No any effect on clearance angle

D] None of them

347] Zero Rake angle give for tool?

A] To avoid friction of tool

B] For increase tool life

C] For increase straight of tool

D] For better finishing on job

348] For carbide tip tool turning on hard material it has.....ecential?

A] Side Rake angle

B] Zero Rake angle

C] Positive Rake angle

D] Negative Rake angle

349] For do not break cutting edge of cutting tool...?

A] Feed increase

B] Cutting speed done low

C] Length of nose decrease

D] Use negative rake angle

350] Chip breaker in a tool is given

A] 'It break the chips into small pieces

B] to have continuous type of chips from long cut

C] to have crushed chips.

351] Step type chip breaker is the one

A] in which a small groove is ground behind the cutting edge

B] in which a step IS ground on the face of the tool along the cutting edge

C] in which a thin carbide plate or clamp is brazed or screwed on the face of the tool.

352] In following which type of tip for cemented carbide treading tool?

A] For clamping on reject tool

B] with brazing on tool

C] With welding on tool

D] With soldering on tool

353] The tip of a cemented carbide threading tool is

A] brazed

B] welded

C] soldered

D] clamped to the shank

354] The cutting speed for aluminium with H.S.S. tools is

A] 30 m/min

B] 50 m/min

C] 70 m/min

D] 130 m/min

355] The cutting speed for brass with a H.S.S. tool is

A] 10 m/min

B] 25 m/min

C] 70 m/min

D] 140 m/min

356] The distance, which the cutting edge of a tool passes over the material in a minute while machining is Know as...

A] RPM

B] Feed

C] Machine speed

D] Cutting speed

357] By using coolants on workpieces we can choose

A] higher cutting speeds

B] lower cutting feeds

C] lower cutting speeds

D] heavy depth of cuts

358] What is a break down maintenance?

A] Maintenance to minimize the unforeseen breakdown

B] Maintenance generally performed by operator himself

C] Maintenance involves replacement of worn out parts

D] Repairs work carried only when machine breakdown

359] Extreme pressure additive (EPA] is mixed with cutting fluid for improving its power of.

A] Cooling

B] Lubrication

D] Production of the machined surface

C] Cleaning of cutting zone

360] The main purpose for using a lubricant in machine tools is to ------

A] Cool down the making parts

B] Prevent machine tool from heating

C] Wet the making parts for close contact

D] Minimize the friction between the making parts

361] Preventive maintenance is ....

A] The maintenance involves the use of sensitive instruments

B] The maintenance generally performed by operator himself

C] The work carried only when machine break down

D] plan to minimize the unforeseen break down

362] What is a break down maintenance?

A] Maintenance to minimize the unforeseen breakdown

B] Maintenance generally performed by operator himself

C] Maintenance involves replacement of worn out parts

D] Repairs work carried only when machine breakdown

363] The Routine Maintenance is ---------

A] it is planned maintenance to minimize the unforeseen breakdown

B] This type of maintenance involves the use of sensitive instrument

C] It is repair work carried only when machine breakdowns

D] This types of maintenance is generally performed by operator himself

364] Lubricant is necessary to ....

A] run the machine smoothly taking least load

B] Run the machine quickly

C] Stop the machine immediately

D] Produce work piece of greater accuracy

365] The main purpose for using a lubricant in machine tools is to ------

A] Cool down the making parts

B] Prevent machine tool from heating

C] Wet the making parts for close contact

D] Minimize the friction between the making parts

Sheet Metal MCQ for Fitter Trade

366] Which method of development is used for developing a rectangular tray?

A] triangular method

B] radial line method

C] parallel line method

D] trial and error method

367] What is the profile of the knife cutting edge of the upper blade of the hand level shear?

A] curved

B] straight

C] inclined

D] beveled

368] For what purpose a groover is used in sheet metal work?

A] to make a hem

B] to make grooves

C] to close and lock the seams

D] to strength then the edge of a job

369] Which type of stake is to be selected for making sharp bends, folding of edges of sheet metal?

A] hatchet stake

B] beak iron stake

C] square edge stake

D] tinman's anvil stake

370] Ammonium chloride is used as a flux for soldering...

A] steel

B] aluminium

C] galvanized iron

D] stainless steel

371] Name the tool used to make and finish the leak proof joints of a pipe T joint

A] groover

B] setting hammer

C] creasing hammer

D] round bottom stake

372] Which one of the following metals will not permit X-rays to pass through?

A] stainless steel

B] aluminium

C] lead

D] tin

373] The frequency of up and down vibration of the cutting edge in a nibbling machine is...

A] 1000 to 1500 times

B] 1500 to 2500 times

C] 2800 to 3000 times

D] 3000 to 3500 times

374] Name the instrument used to check the perpendicularity of the branch pipe with the main pipe of a pipe T joint

A] protractor

B] try square

C] spirit level

D] straight edge

375].Which type of notch is used when a single hem meets at right angles?

A] V notch

B] slit notch

C] slant notch

D] square notch

376] To cut out small apertures which punch and die type of machine is used?

A] shear type nibbler

B] punch type nibbler

C] circular cutting machine

D] guillotine shearing machine

377] The overheating of the blow pipe nozzle is to be avoided because it will

A] cause back fire

B] consume more oxygen and acetylene

C] create burn through defect in the joint

D] create undercut defect in the joint

378] State the nozzle size you will select to weld a 3.15mm thick mild steel sheet

A] 3

B.5

C] 7

D] 10

379] The type of flame to be set for welding brass is...

A] air acetylene flame

B] neutral flame

C] oxidizing flame

D] carburizing flame

380] What is the maximum thickness of mild steel sheet recommended for gas welding using leftward technique?

A] 12mm

B] 10mm

C] 8mm

D] 5mm

381].The distance between the root and toe of a fillet weld is called...

A] root gap

B] leg length

C] reinforcement

D] throat thickness

382] Name the weld defect which occurs due to improper cleaning of the mild steel sheet edge and surface

A] lack of root penetration

B] burn through

C] undercut

D] <u>porosity</u>

383] Which of the following mechanical properties of metals gives resistance to pulling forces?

A] toughness

B] ductility

C] hardness

D] <u>tensile strength</u>

INDUSTRIAL TRAINING INSTITUTE

Monthly Test-1, Marks- 20, Date:- ________________

(Every Question Carry Two Marks)

01] In case of bleeding, take treatment Of

A] spray cold water

B] Bandage immediately -----]

C] Enquire about the accident thought treatment

D] cold 3" and rest

02] in case of an accident, the victim should im

A] Asked to take rest

C] Attended immediately

D] leave him

03] First aid is given to an injured or ill person primarily....

A] Save life

B] Prevent further deterioration of the muff's

C] Give best possible comfort

D] All of these

04] Colour code for Bins for waste paper segregation is -----

A] blue Colour

B] Yellow Colour

C] Red Colour

D] Green Colour

05] In Japanese Seiko stands for --------------

A] Shine

B] Sort

C] Standardize

D] Sustain

06] Benefit of SS system is ------

A] Increase in productivity

B] Increase in quality

C] Reduction in wastage of time

D] All of these

07] Safety is -----------

A] nobody's business

B] every bodise business

C] Some bodies business

D] The organization business

08] For basic categories of safety signs are available The meaning of"prohibition" sign ----

A] shows it must not be done

B] Shows what must be done

C] Warns the hazard or danger

D] Gives information of safety provision

09] Which one is a workshop safety?

A] Keep shop floor clean and free from grease, oil or other slippery materials

B] Stop the machine before changing the speed

C] Don't use cracked or chipped tools

D] Don't try to stop a running machine with hand

10] In Personal Protect Equipment (PPE] HELMET is used to

A] protect head

B] Protect eyes

C] Protect hands

D] Protect ears

INDUSTRIAL TRAINING INSTITUTE

Monthly Test-2, Marks- 20, Date:- _______________

(Every Question Carry Two Marks)

1- 17] Which type of fire extinguisher is used to put off general fire?

A] Water type Extinguisher

B] Foam type Extinguisher

C] Dry chemical powder Extinguisher

D] Carbon dioxide (C02] Extinguisher

2-18] One micrometer (U] is equal to...

A] 0.1mm

B] 0.01mm

C] 0.001mm

D] 0.0001mm

3-19] Name the tool used to make and finish the leak proof joints of a pipe T joint

A] groover

B] setting hammer

C] creasing hammer

D] round bottom stake

4-20] Portion of the hammer used for fixing the handle is...

A] Face

B] Peen

C] Chcek

D] Eye hole

5-21] Weight of the hammer for the marking purpose is...

A] 250g

B] 500g

C] 1 kg

D] 2 kgs

6-22] To cut out small apertures which punch and die type of machine is used?

A] shear type nibbler

B] punch type nibbler

C] circular cutting machine

D] guillotine shearing machine

7-23] Scribers are made of...

A] Mild steel

B] High carbon steel

C] Brass

D] Cast iron

8-24] The size of an engineer's vice is specified by the...

A] Length of the movable jaw

B] Width of the jaws

C] Height of the vice

D] Maximum opening of the jaws

9-25] The form of thread used in carpenters vice is...

A] Square

B] Acme thread

C] Sawtooth Thread

D] Knuckle thread

10-26] The convexity of files helps...

A] To file concave surfaces

B] To file convex surfaces

C] To prevent rounding of edges of work

D] The file to become straight when pressure is applied

INDUSTRIAL TRAINING INSTITUTE

Monthly Test-3, Marks- 20, Date:- _______________

(Every Question Carry Two Marks)

1-33] The reason for using cast iron in making 'V' blocks

A] to increase the weight of the block

B] to reduce the cost

C] to reduce the friction

D] to get a good appearance

2-34] For cutting thin tubing, the most suitable pitch of the hacksaw blade is...

A] 1.8mm

B] 1.4mm

C] 1mm

D] 0.8mm

3-35] For cutting solid brass, the most suitable pitch of the hacksaw blade is...

A] 1.8mm

B] 1.4mm

C] 1mm

D] 0.8mm

4-36] A new hacksaw blade after a few strokes becomes loose because of the...

A] Stretching of the blade

B] Wing-nut threads being worn out

C] Wrong pitch of the blade

D] Improper selection of the set of saws.

5-37] While cutting small diameter pipes, it is advisable to watch regularly and ensure that...

A] The cut is along the curved line

B] More saw teeth are in contract

C] The work is not overheated

D] Proper balancing of hacksaw is maintained

6-38] If the drill runs untrue, it will

A] get too hot

B] cut undersize

C] distort the spindle

D] cut an oversized hole

7-39] Running the drill too fast many result in

A] spoiling the cutting edge

B] poor surface finish

C] twisting the tang

D] drilling an oval hole

8-40] A drill with worn land will

A] drill hole oversize

B] drill hole undersize

C] run out of centre

D] drill an accurate hole

9-41] The morse taper provided on drills used on lathe ranges between

A] MT1 to MT5

B] MT1 to MT4

C] MT0 to MT5

D] MT0 to MT4

10-42] Feeding the small drill too fast into the work may result in

A] breaking the drill

B] bending the drill

C] cutting an oval shape hole

D] increased production

INDUSTRIAL TRAINING INSTITUTE

Monthly Test-4, Marks- 20, Date:- _______________

(Every Question Carry Two Marks)

1-50] The point angle of drills depends on...

A] The size of the drill

B] The type of machine

C] The material of the work

D] The RPM of the drill

2-51] The point angle for a standard drill is...

A] 60°

B] 108°

C] <u>118°</u>

D] 135°

3-52] The helical angle determines the...

A] Cutting angle

B] Chew angle

C] <u>Rake angle</u>

D] Lip angle

4-53] The clearance angle of the drill is between...

A] 3° to 5°

B] <u>8° to 12°</u>

C] 12° to 20°

D] 15° to 20°

5-54] The relief angle provided behind the cutting edge is called the..

A] Point angle

B] Chisel edge angle

C] Helix angle

D] <u>Clearance angle</u>

6-55] A set of number drill series consists of drills in the following ranges] Indicate the correct range

A] 1 to 40

B] 1 to 50

C] <u>1 to 80</u>

D] 1 to 100

7-56] In the number drill series, the smallest drill size is...

A] 0.1 mm

B] <u>0.35 mm</u>

C] 0.5 mm

D] 0.52 mm

8-57] In the number drill series, the largest drill size is...

A] 102 mm

B] <u>5.791 mm</u>

C] 5.613 mm

D] 5.410 mm

9-58] In the letter drill series, the size of the drill 'A' is equal to ...

A] 13 mm

B] 6.08 mm

C] 6.045 mm

D] 5.944 mm

10-59] In the letter drill series, the largest drill size is equal to...

A] 10.33 mm

B] 10.490 mm

C] 12.01 mm

D] 15.00 mm

INDUSTRIAL TRAINING INSTITUTE

Monthly Test-5, Marks- 20, Date:- _______________

(Every Question Carry Two Marks)

1-66] which one of the following is the most suitable tap for lathe work?

A] spiral tap

B] machine tap

C] hand tap

D] left hand tap

2-67] A die is turned with a

A] die wrench

B] diestock

C] die plate

D] die handle

3-68] A tumbler gear unit has

A] a single gear

B] two gears

C] three gears

D] four gears

4-69] The cutting edge of a solid tool is made of

A] carbon steel

B] mild steel

C] super high speed steel

D] stelite

5-70] The tip of a cemented carbide threading tool is

A] brazed

B] welded

C] soldered

D] clamped to the shank

6-71] Tool will rub against the work surfaces and the cutting force increases when..

A] The clearance angle is more

B] The clearance angel is less

C] The rake angle is more

D] The rake angle is less

7-72] Formation of a chip while cutting is based on the...

A] Rake angle of the tool

B] Clearance angle of the tool

C] Wedge angle of the tool

D] Clearance and wedge angle of the tool

8-73] The suitable cutting fluid for drilling mild steel in a drilling machine is...

A] Synthetic soluble oil

B] Neat oil

C] Distilled water

D] Soluble oil

9-74] Centre drilling is an operation of...

A] Drilling and countersinking

B] Drilling and counter boring

C] Marking the centre location before drilling

D] Enlarging the diameter of a hole

10-75] Shaft ends are centre drilled for...

A] Supporting jobs between centres

B] Lubricating the dead centre

C] Reducing the weight

D] Assisting counter boring

INDUSTRIAL TRAINING INSTITUTE

Monthly Test-6, Marks- 20, Date:- _______________

(Every Question Carry Two Marks)

1-80] The process of enlarging the end of a hole for accommodating the socket screw head is...

A] Reaming

B] Spot facing

C] Counter boring

D] Counter sinking

2-81]While choosing a boring tool for boring a given diameter, select

A] a long tool

B] a short tool

C] a long and stout tool

D] a short and stout tool

3-82] The cutting edge of the boring tool should be set for a small hole so that it is

A] 0.5 mm above the center

B] 0.5 mm below the center

C] 1 mm above the center

D] in the exact center

4-83] Bored holes are to be chamfered by using

A] a drill

B] triangular scraper

C] a cranked boring tool

D] a flat file

5-84] The tool used for boring deep holes is a

A] lathe mandrel

B] sleeve

C] drill

D] auger bit

6-85] The cutting speed for rough boring is the

A] same as rough turning

B] same as drilling

C] same as knurling

D] same as thread cutting

7-86] The reamer is used for...

A] Drilling holes in thin sheets

B] Drilling deep holes

C] Removing burrs

D] Enlarging and finishing holes

8-87] The reamer teeth are unevenly spaced because...

A] They are easy to manufacture

B] They can reduce chattering

C] They help to cut metal gradually

D] They help to remove the reamer easily

9-88] Which among the following is not a capability of reamers?

A] Finishing small holes

B] Finishing any machined profiles

C] Accuracy to closer limits

D] Producing high quality surface finish

10-89] The most important quality of any cutting fluid is

A] emulsification

B] specific heat

C] specific gravity

D] viscosity

INDUSTRIAL TRAINING INSTITUTE

Monthly Test-7, Marks- 20, Date:- ______________

(Every Question Carry Two Marks)

1-95] The depth of cut is given by

A] the top slide

B] the cross-slide

C] the compound slide

D] adjusting the tool

2-96] For mounting a lathe chuck

A] start it by hand and then turn the power on

B] mount it on by power

C] mount it by hand

D] mount it with the help of a hammer

3-97] The morse taper provided on drills used on lathe ranges between

A] MT1 to MT5

B] MT1 to MT4

C] MT0 to MT5

D] MT0 to MT4

4-98] Feeding the small drill too fast into the work may result in

A] breaking the drill

B] bending the drill

C] cutting an oval shape hole

D] increased production

5-99] Number of flutes in a twist drills are --------

A] 1

B] 2

C] 3

D] 4

6-100] Which one of the following drilling machines is used for drilling holes where electricity is not available?

A] Bench drilling machine

B] Pillar drilling machine

C] Redial drilling machine

D] Ratchet drilling machine

7-101] Which one of the following drilling machine is used for heavy duty work?

A] Bench drilling machine

B] Pillar drilling machine

C] Radial drilling machine

D] Electric hand drilling machine

8-102] The suitable cutting fluid for drilling mild steel in a lathe is

A] synthetic soluble oil

B] neat cutting oil

C] distilled water

D] soluble oil+water

9-103] The suitable cutting fluid for precision grinding is

A] Soluble oil

B] Synthetic soluble oil

C] Neat oil

D] Servo Cut's'

10-104] Advantage of using cutting fluid during grinding operation is ------

A] 5000 surface finish

B] Reduction in cutting forces

C] Reduction in hardening of the work piece

D] All of these]

INDUSTRIAL TRAINING INSTITUTE

Monthly Test-8, Marks- 20, Date:- ________________

(Every Question Carry Two Marks)

1-110] Which is correct angle plate used with face plate

(A] Solid Type

(B] Box Type

(C] Adjustable Type

(D] None of them

2-111] Face plate is made from.....]

(A] Mild Steel

(B] Cast Iron

(C] Brass

(D] Aluminium

3-112] Which following accessories is use for odd an uneven job turning?

(A] Three Jaw Chuck

(B] Two Jaw Chuck

(C] Driving Plate

(D] Face Plate

4-113] An irregular shaped work piece is turned on a Lathe] Which one of the following work holding accessories is used?

A] Two Jaw chuck

B] Three Jaw chuck

C] Driving plate

D] Face plate

5-114]The pads of a steady rest are made of

A] carbon steel

B] lead

C] mild steel

D] brass

6-115] A steady rest is used

A] to hold jobs

B] for face plate work

C] to drive the job

D] to support the job

7-116] A follower steady is held on the

A] lathe bed

B] lathe carriage

C] lathe spindle

D] tailstock

8-117] When turning long work pieces, the following is used

A sleeve

B change gear

C steady rest

D bracket]

9-118] Knurling operation is done at the

A] turning spindle speed

B] high spindle speed

C] 1/3 of the turning spindle speed

D] 1⁄2 of the turning spindle speed

10-119] Knurling is the operation of

A] shearing

B] forming

C] turning

D] pressing

INDUSTRIAL TRAINING INSTITUTE

Monthly Test-9, Marks- 20, Date:- _______________

(Every Question Carry Two Marks)

1-125] The number of fundamental deviations in the B.I.S] system are

A] 20

B] 22

C] 25

D] 28

2-126] The number of grade of tolerances in the B.I.S] system are

A] 12

B] 16

C] 18

D] 20

3-127] The size based on which the dimensional deviations are given is called...

A] Actual size

B] Basic size

C] Minimum limit of size

D] Maximum limit of Size

4-128] The size of parts made by .....] for provide interchange ability properties] (A] Measurement System

(B] Trial and Error System

(C] Limit and Tolerance System

(D] None of Them

5-129] Your job taper is correct if it is measured

A above the higher limit

B in between higher and lower limit

C below the lower limit]

6-130] When tolerance given in one side of the basic dimension, it is called --------

A].Tolerance system

B] Unilateral tolerance

C] Bilateral tolerance

D] Allowance System

**7-131] A dimension is stated as (025 H7 in a drawing] The lower limit is -----------

A] 24.75 mm

B] 24.85 mm

C] 25.00 mm

D] 25-021 mm

**8-132] The measured Size Of the dimensions of a component as called---------

A] Basic size

B] Nominal Size

C] Allowed size

D] Actual size

9-133] In the drawing the dimensions of a shaft is shown 40i 0068/ 0042, which is the size of Shaft within the tolerance?

A] 4.0.64 mm

B] 40.042 mm

C] 40.000 mm

D] 39.998 mm

10-134] In Hole basic system ----------

A] The size of the shaft is made constant

B] The Size of the hole is made constant

C] Only 'allowance is given on the hole

INDUSTRIAL TRAINING INSTITUTE

Monthly Test-10, Marks- 20, Date:- ________________

(Every Question Carry Two Marks)

1-142] A Product is said to have the quality when ....]

A] Its shape and dimensions are within the limit

B] It is fit for use

C] It appears to be very good

D] The choice of material is right

2-143] The maximum clearance required between hole'30 +0.021, 0.000 and shaft 30 -0.110, 0.143 is.

A] 0.110 mm '

B]0.131 mm

C] 0.164 mm

D] 0.143 mm

3-144] A dimension is stated as 25 .1002 mm in a drawing] What is the tolerance?

A] +0.02 mm'

B] +0.04 mm

C] -0.02 mm

D] 25.00 mm

4-145] A pin is fitted in a hole] The tolerance zone of the pin is entirely above that of hole] The fit obtained will be?

A] Clearance fit

B] Transition fit

C] Interference fit

D] Running fit

5-146] Interchange ability is normally applied for? _

A] Repairing of parts

B] Mass production

C] Single piece production

D] All of these

6-147] Tolerance is given to the part size to...........]

A] Production the part within the required permissible size error

B] Increase the production

C] Decrease the Production

D] Finish the components approximately

7-148] Which one of the following is the clearance fit under the whole basic system?

A] 20 H7/p6'

B] 2067/211

C] ZOG/gll]

D] 20H/g11]

8-149] The three classes of fits as per BIS system aré ....] ~]

A] Clearance fit, interference fit and transition fit

B] Medium fit, push fit and tight fit

C] Flat fit, round fit and square fit

D] 'Sliding fit ', loose fit and shrinkage fit

9-150] Which one of the following tolerance specifications has a maximum dimensionless than 20 mm?

A] 20 +0.2,-0.3

B] 20 320.2

C] 20 -0.2, 0.3 e

D]m 20 +500, ~03

10-151] Difference between the maximum and minimum limit is -~-~~~~-~~~~ '

A] Single informant

B] Basic shaft

C] Clearance

D] Tolerance

INDUSTRIAL TRAINING INSTITUTE

Monthly Test-11, Marks- 20, Date:- _______________

(Every Question Carry Two Marks)

1-160] The length of turned tapers are checked with

A vernier calliper

B micrometer

C inside callper

D dial test indicator]

2-161] The disadvantages of taper turning using the com] pound slide are

A] only long tapers can be turned

B] only very large tapers can be turned

C] only manual in feed is possible

D] only short tapers can be turned due to the restrictions of the compound slide]

3-162] External tapers are checked with

A] limit plug gauge

B] taper ring gauge

C]taper plug gauge

D] thread plug gauge]

4-163] The use of a taper turned on lathe is ----

A] Assist to transmit drive in the assembled parts

B] Used for Assembly and disassembly of parts

C] Give self alignment in the assembled parts

5-164] Which type of method is used in mass production of production of producing small length of taper?

A] Form tool

B] Compound slide

C] Tailstock offset.

D] Taper turning attachment

6-165] Morse standard taper is one of the internationally accepted standards taper, which is available in numbers from--------

A]1to7

B]1 to 8

C] O to 7

D] 0 to 8

7-166] Which taper turning method is used for cutting steep taper?

A] Set over method

B] Taper turning attachment

C] Form tool

D] Swivelling the compound rest

8-167] Morse taper is used in which of the following machine components -...

A] Spindles of lathe

B] Spindles of drill machine

C] Shanks of reamers

D] All of these

9-168] For mass production of the taper which one of the following method is used.......]

A] Tailstock offset method

B] Taper turning attachment method

C] Form too method

D] Compound slide method

10-169] The major diameter of the taper is 40 mm, minor diameter is 30 mm] The total length of the job is 100 mm is tapered then offset is given by -

A] 5 mm

B] 7.5 mm

C] 12 mm

D] 9 mm

INDUSTRIAL TRAINING INSTITUTE

Monthly Test-12, Marks- 20, Date:- _______________

(Every Question Carry Two Marks)

1-190] Which instrument iis used for marking layout?

A] Micrometer

B] Vernier

C] Depth gauge

D] Vernier height gauge

2-191] While marking with a Vernier height gauge, the work piece is generally ----------

A] Supported by an angle plate
B] Supported by another work piece
C] Held by one hand
D] Held without support
3-192] Which of the following is not the part of a combination set?
A] Stock
B] Square head
C] Protractor head
D] Centre head
4-193] A BSW threading tool is to be ground with an included angle of
A] 55°
B] 60°
C] 47.5°
D] 29°
5-194] The nose radius of a metric 'V' thread tool is
A] 0.144 x P
B] 0.25 x P
C] 0.414 x P
D] 0.0144 x P
6-195] While cutting metric external threads of coarse pitches, it is advisable to swivel the compound rest to
A] 45°
B] 30°
C] 60°
D.90°
7-196] The depth of B.I.S] metric thread is
A] 0.6403 x P
B] 0.6 x P
C] 0.6134 x P
D] 0.5 x P
8-197] Threading tools are checked for accuracy for the 60° angle by using a
A] Thread plug gauge
B] centre gauge
C] screw pitch gauge
D] tool angle gauge
9-198] The number of threads per inch can be checked with a

A] tool gauge
B] metric rule by counting
C] ring gauge
D] screw pitch gauge
10-199] When threading, the carriage is moved along the ways by
A] a gear train on a track
B] the feed rod spline or key-way
C] the lead screw thred
D] the hand wheel